Steve Moyise is Professor of New Testament at the University of Chichester. He is author of *The Old Testament in the Book of Revelation* (1995), *The Old Testament in the New* (2001), *Evoking Scripture: Seeing the Old Testament in the New* (2008) and *Paul and Scripture* (SPCK 2010). He is also co-editor with Maarten Menken of a series of books looking at the way particular Old Testament books are used in the New Testament, including *Psalms in the New Testament* (2004), *Isaiah in the New Testament* (2005), *Deuteronomy in the New Testament* (2007) and *The Minor Prophets in the New Testament* (2009).

JESUS AND SCRIPTURE

STEVE MOYISE

First published in Great Britain in 2010

Society for Promoting Christian Knowledge
36 Causton Street
London SW1P 4ST
www.spckpublishing.co.uk

British Library Cataloguing-in-Publication Data
A catalogue record for this book is available from the British Library

ISBN 978–0–281–06217–1

1 3 5 7 9 10 8 6 4 2

Typeset by Graphicraft Ltd, Hong Kong
Printed in Great Britain by the MPG Books Group

Produced on paper from sustainable forests

Contents

Contents

Contents

Abbreviations

CD	*Damascus Document*
ConBNT	Coniectanea biblica, New Testament Series
JSNT	*Journal for the Study of the New Testament*
JSNTSup	*Journal for the Study of the New Testament*, Supplement Series
JSOTSup	*Journal for the Study of the Old Testament*, Supplement Series
KJV	King James Version
LXX	Septuagint (Greek translation)
m.	Mishnah
NETS	New English Translation of the Septuagint
NIGTC	New International Greek Testament Commentary
NIV	New International Version
NJB	New Jerusalem Bible
NovT	*Novum Testamentum*
NovTSup	*Novum Testamentum*, Supplements
NRSV	New Revised Standard Version
NTS	*New Testament Studies*
RSV	Revised Standard Version
SNTSMS	Society for New Testament Studies Monograph Series
WUNT	Wissenschaftliche Untersuchungen zum Neuen Testament

Introduction

Jesus was a Jew, and like other Jews he was brought up to believe that the Scriptures of Israel were not simply human wisdom but a gift from God. Tradition held that Moses ascended Mount Sinai and brought back the Ten Commandments, along with a host of other laws now recorded in the Torah (Hebrew name) or Pentateuch (Greek name). We know the books as Genesis, Exodus, Leviticus, Numbers and Deuteronomy, and together they formed the foundation of Jewish life. Christians are inclined to think of the numerous laws as a burden, but the Jews thought otherwise: 'The law of the LORD is perfect, reviving the soul; the decrees of the LORD are sure, making wise the simple; the precepts of the LORD are right, rejoicing the heart; the commandment of the LORD is clear, enlightening the eyes' (Ps. 19.7–8). There are verses in the Gospels where Jesus expresses a similar view (Matt. 5.17–19; Mark 7.9–13).

Along with the Torah, or law, Jewish tradition recognized a second group of writings, known as the prophets. This was divided into the former prophets (Joshua, Judges, Samuel, Kings) and the latter prophets (Isaiah, Jeremiah, Ezekiel, the Twelve). In many ways these books were regarded as commentary on the law, either telling the story of Israel and its relationship with the law (the covenant), or speaking out when Israel or (more often) its leaders were failing to keep it. It was because of such failures that the prophets began to speak of a new age when righteousness and justice would prevail (Isa. 1.26–27). Such hopes were diverse, some pointing to a glorious future for Israel (Isa. 60.19–22), some to universal peace (Isa. 11.1–9) and others to a completely new heaven and earth (Isa. 65.17). Scripture was often referred to as 'the law and the prophets'.

A third group was simply known as the writings. Many of the books are what we would call wisdom (Proverbs, Job, Ecclesiastes), but the most important book was Psalms. The fact that it is divided into five books (1—41, 42—72, 73—89, 90—106, 107—150) like the five books of Moses is indicative of its importance for Israel. Not only does it contain hymns and laments for public worship, it also provides the language of private prayer. It is widely quoted throughout the

1

New Testament and, as we shall see, was particularly important for Jesus. The writings also contains books like Ruth and Daniel, which later collections (like the Greek Bible) would place after Judges and Ezekiel respectively. Many scholars believe this third section was still in a state of flux at the time of Jesus, and it is interesting that Luke ends his Gospel with Jesus declaring: 'These are my words that I spoke to you while I was still with you – that everything written about me in the law of Moses, the prophets, and the psalms must be fulfilled' (Luke 24.44). It is possible that 'psalms' here stands for 'writings' (as its prominent member), but it may equally suggest that the third section of the Hebrew Bible was yet to be finalized.

The Jews of Jesus' day spoke Aramaic, but nearly all of these books were written in Hebrew. Thus when the Scriptures were read in the synagogues there was a need to translate them into Aramaic, and the name given to these translations was Targum (plural Targumim). Most of the Targumim that have come down to us are from a much later period, and it used to be thought that they were only known in oral form in Jesus' day. However, we have now found fragments of Targumim among the Dead Sea Scrolls (Leviticus and Job), proving that at least some of them were written documents in the first century CE. What is interesting about this is that when we compare these Aramaic translations with the Hebrew texts, they are more like paraphrases than literal translations. For example, the first phrase of Genesis 2.7 ('the LORD God formed man from the dust of the ground') has been greatly expanded in *Targum Pseudo-Jonathan* to: 'And the Lord God created man in two formations; and took dust from the place of the house of the sanctuary, and from the four winds of the world, and mixed from all the waters of the world, and created him red, black and white'. Although there are no examples in the Gospels of Jesus quoting such expansions, there is evidence that he was sometimes influenced by their wording.

However, of much greater significance for our study is the fact that the principal sources for our knowledge of Jesus (Matthew, Mark, Luke and John) were written in Greek, including the sayings of Jesus (with a few exceptions like *ephphatha* in Mark 7.34 and *talitha cum* in Mark 5.41, where the Aramaic has been preserved). At some point in the transmission of Jesus' sayings they were translated into Greek, including his quotations from Scripture. Now this presents a particular difficulty because the Hebrew Scriptures had already been translated

into Greek, a version known as the Septuagint (often abbreviated to
LXX, a usage we shall follow throughout this book),[1] and like the
Targumim it does not always agree with the Hebrew text. In fact
the accuracy of the translation varies greatly from book to book. In the
Torah, or law, the translation is fairly literal, but in the wisdom books
the differences can be quite extensive. The important question this
raises is whether, when the translators recognized that Jesus was
quoting Scripture, they translated his words for themselves or availed
themselves of the translation already in circulation. In cases where
the LXX offers a literal translation of the Hebrew there is no way of
telling, but in cases where it differs from the Hebrew the evidence
suggests that the translators usually availed themselves of the LXX – or
a revision of it – rather than offer their own translations.[2]

New English Translation of the LXX (NETS)

There have until very recently been only two translations of the
LXX into English, those of the American scholar Charles Thomson
(1808) and the English cleric Sir Lancelot Brenton (1844). But
in 2007 a group of scholars used the latest manuscript evidence
to produce NETS. This is an extremely useful resource for two
reasons. First, each book or section of the LXX is introduced by
a short essay on the characteristics of its original translator.
Second, it has adopted the strategy of conforming the translation
to the NRSV whenever the Greek and Hebrew are close, and
departing from it when they are not. Thus the English reader
can compare the NRSV – which is a translation of the Hebrew
text – and NETS and get some impression of the similarities and
differences between the Greek and Hebrew versions, and of the
effect of these on the meaning of the text. For example, the
Hebrew of Isaiah 29.13 makes the following accusation of Israel:
'their worship of me is a human commandment learned by rote'.
The LXX has rendered this: 'in vain do they worship me, teaching
human precepts and teachings', and this is the form quoted in
Mark 7.6–7 (see page 21).

The evidence of the Gospels

The four Gospels found in the New Testament present Jesus as
quoting from nearly 60 different verses of Scripture and making at

least twice that number of allusions and more general references. The popular view is that Jesus frequently quoted from the prophets, but there are in fact more references to the law (26) and the writings (16) than to the prophets (15 – including one from Daniel, which appears among the prophets in the LXX but among the writings in the Hebrew Bible). The distribution is interesting. The quotations from the law are drawn from Deuteronomy (11) and Exodus (8), with only three from each of Genesis and Leviticus and one from Numbers. From the prophets it is principally Isaiah (7), with two from Hosea and one from each of Jeremiah, Daniel, Jonah, Micah, Zechariah and Malachi. From the writings, all are from Psalms (and one from Daniel). This distribution resembles that of the Qumran community (from which come the Dead Sea Scrolls), where the most quoted books are Psalms, Isaiah and Deuteronomy.

To those unaccustomed to modern biblical studies, it might be thought that our next step is simply to examine each of these verses (in context) and then draw conclusions about Jesus' use of Scripture. However, the nature of the Gospels means that our task is rather more complicated than that. For example, if we look at the story narrated in Mark 12.28–34, we see that Jesus responds to the question of which is the greatest commandment (Mark 12.28) by saying: 'The first is, "Hear, O Israel: the Lord our God, the Lord is one; you shall love the Lord your God with all your heart, and with all your soul, and with all your mind, and with all your strength." The second is this, "You shall love your neighbour as yourself." There is no other commandment greater than these' (Mark 12.29–31). Many have thought this to be a mark of Jesus' genius. Not only does he give the 'standard' answer (to love God) but he couples it with the command to love neighbour, thereby ensuring that religious zeal is never at the expense of social concern. However, before we get too excited about discovering the key to Jesus' use of Scripture, we need to look at an earlier story that occurs in Luke:

> Just then a lawyer stood up to test Jesus. 'Teacher,' he said, 'what must I do to inherit eternal life?' He said to him, 'What is written in the law? What do you read there?' He answered, 'You shall love the Lord your God with all your heart, and with all your soul, and with all your strength, and with all your mind; and your neighbour as yourself.' And he said to him, 'You have given the right answer; do this, and you will live.'
> (Luke 10.25–28)

In this story it is the lawyer who is the genius who brings together the two commandments, not Jesus. But it does not end there. Luke tells us that the lawyer asked a further question: 'And who is my neighbour?' (Luke 10.29), to which Jesus replied by telling the parable of the Good Samaritan:

> A man was going down from Jerusalem to Jericho, and fell into the hands of robbers, who stripped him, beat him, and went away, leaving him half dead. Now by chance a priest was going down that road; and when he saw him, he passed by on the other side. So likewise a Levite, when he came to the place and saw him, passed by on the other side. But a Samaritan while travelling came near him; and when he saw him, he was moved with pity. He went to him and bandaged his wounds, having poured oil and wine on them. Then he put him on his own animal, brought him to an inn, and took care of him. The next day he took out two denarii, gave them to the innkeeper, and said, 'Take care of him; and when I come back, I will repay you whatever more you spend.' (Luke 10.30–35)

Jesus then challenges the lawyer by asking him which of the three acted as neighbour to the man, a question that the lawyer is forced to answer: 'The one who showed him mercy' (Luke 10.37). Thus Luke agrees with Mark that the question about the greatest commandment provides an illustration of the genius of Jesus' teaching, but does so in a very different way. For Mark, it is the bringing together of the two commandments; if this were the only Gospel we possessed we would conclude that Jesus was the first to do so. However, Luke suggests that the lawyer could do this without even pausing for thought, suggesting that it was a commonplace. For Luke, the genius of Jesus in this incident was not his use of Scripture but the telling of a poignant parable.

This example suggests that in order to describe Jesus' use of Scripture we must attend to two tasks. First, we must study what each Gospel writer has to say about Jesus' use of Scripture and seek to determine his method and purpose. Thus if we had not gone on to read the parable of the Good Samaritan we would have seriously misunderstood Jesus' response to the lawyer. Second, if we are to understand Jesus' use of Scripture we must engage in historical criticism to decide what Jesus *must* have said to give rise to the various accounts we find in the Gospels. Of course, there will be some examples where the Gospels are largely in agreement, but there are

Table I.1

Matthew 27.46	Mark 15.34	Luke 23.46	John 19.30
And about three o'clock Jesus cried with a loud voice, 'Eli, Eli, lema sabachthani?' that is, 'My God, my God, why have you forsaken me?'	At three o'clock Jesus cried out with a loud voice, 'Eloi, Eloi, lema sabachthani?' which means, 'My God, my God, why have you forsaken me?'	Then Jesus, crying with a loud voice, said, 'Father, into your hands I commend my spirit.' Having said this, he breathed his last.	When Jesus had received the wine, he said, 'It is finished.' Then he bowed his head and gave up his spirit.

others where they are not. To illustrate this, consider the final words of Jesus from the cross as shown in Table I.1.

Matthew and Mark are virtually identical except that Matthew's 'Eli, Eli' represents the Hebrew of 'My God, my God', while Mark has the Aramaic. It is a quotation of Psalm 22.1 and thus relevant to our study. Matthew and Mark both think that Jesus ended his life by identifying with David's cry of agony in Psalm 22.1. The only issue is whether Jesus said the words in Hebrew or Aramaic. Luke also thinks that Jesus ended his life with a quotation of Scripture, in this case Psalm 31.5. However, the content of the passage in Luke is very different. Luke presents Jesus as dying in faith and offering his spirit to God, rather than crying out in despair or perhaps even anger. Which is more likely to be true? John is different again. Here there is no quotation of Scripture, but the words 'and gave up his spirit' have a similar function to Luke's quotation. It is important to realize that the questions we are raising do not spring from a particular 'sceptical' or 'unbelieving' approach to Scripture; they arise because of what we find in Scripture and our desire to know the precise words that were spoken.

- Did Jesus end his life by quoting words from Scripture (Matthew/ Mark/Luke) or not (John)?
- If he did, was its content that of reverent submission (Luke) or agony and despair (Matthew/Mark)?
- If it was from Psalm 22.1, did he utter the words in Hebrew or Aramaic?

One response to these differences is to conclude that Jesus must have said all of the sayings and that each Gospel has been selective in what it records. I will call this the 'maximalist' approach as its strategy for dealing with differences between the Gospels is to seek harmony. Its rationale is twofold. First, it is clear that Jesus must have said a great deal more than what we have in the Gospels, so it is quite plausible that each Gospel represents only a selection of what Jesus said. Second, a historian will generally try and use as much of the available evidence as possible in reconstructing the past. Any theory that involves discounting 50 per cent or even 75 per cent of the available evidence does not command much confidence.

On the other hand, there are difficulties with such a view. First, although it suggests that it is simply taking the evidence at face value, it cannot avoid constructing hypotheses of its own. For example, if Jesus is thought to have said all of the above sayings, a decision still has to be made as to which is the final saying. The question is not trivial, as film makers have shown. Did Jesus cry out in agony in the early stages of the crucifixion (Matthew/Mark) but accept his fate towards the end (Luke), eventually realizing that his work on earth was complete (John)? Or did Jesus begin with trust (Luke) and believe his work was done (John), but as the agony of the crucifixion increased, end his life by crying out in despair (Matthew/Mark)? The point is that the 'maximalist' approach has not really solved the difficulty; it has merely transferred it to another place.

Second, the maximalist approach raises difficult questions about the integrity of the Gospel writers. If Jesus did in fact say all of these sayings and the sequence was that he ended his life in despair (Matthew/Mark), then is not Luke being rather misleading by only quoting the positive saying? Of course, Luke doesn't actually deny that Jesus spoke of being forsaken, so one could argue that he is not technically at fault. But does his silence not amount to misrepresentation? Readers of Luke would come away with the view that Jesus ended his life in reverent submission, with no hint of the despair recorded in Matthew and Mark.

The Synoptic problem

For over two centuries scholars have been trying to determine the relationship between the Gospels. Anyone who reads the Gospels carefully will soon discover that Matthew, Mark and Luke have much in common but John is very different. With the exception of the feeding of the 5,000 and the walking on water, John has a completely different set of miracle stories from the other three Gospels, which became known as the Synoptic Gospels (meaning they can be seen together). John is seen by most scholars as the latest of the Gospels, and contains a great deal of theological reflection on such themes as Jesus' pre-existence, incarnation and divinity.

This contrast is easily seen by considering how each Gospel begins. Mark begins with the adult Jesus coming to John for baptism and experiencing the descent of the Spirit, which empowers him for a ministry of teaching and healing. Readers of Mark have no reason to think that Jesus was anything 'special' before this event. In contrast, both Matthew and Luke begin with two chapters of nativity stories that show that Jesus had a miraculous birth (by the Holy Spirit). This explains why he grew up to have a ministry of teaching and healing; he was 'special' from the moment of conception. However, while readers of Matthew and Luke have no reason to conclude that Jesus had an existence before his birth, this is precisely what the opening chapter of John states. Jesus was in the beginning with God but also 'became flesh and lived among us' (John 1.14). And it is from this perspective that John tells his story of Jesus, so that the meaning of the words 'It is finished' is that Jesus came from God to do the will of God and is now returning (John 17.1–5).[3]

Now while we are not to imagine that the Gospels represent three stages of theological development (Jesus as empowered human, Jesus as miraculous human, Jesus as divine human), most scholars do believe that Mark was the earliest Gospel (*c.* 65 CE), that it was followed by Matthew and Luke (*c.* 75–85 CE) and that John was the latest (*c.* 95 CE). The reasons for this can be found in most introductions to the Gospels and need not detain us further.[4] When applied to Jesus' final words on the cross, this understanding suggests that Mark is closest to what Jesus actually said. This is reproduced by Matthew, except that he changes the Aramaic saying ('Eloi, eloi') to the Hebrew ('Eli, eli'), either because he thought it more apt that Jesus would quote the Hebrew text or because he thought it better explains the confusion with the name 'Elijah' that follows. Luke has a different purpose for writing his Gospel and wishes to emphasize how Jesus lived his life in service for others. He thus substitutes for Psalm 22.1 a different psalm of David – Psalm

31.5. John is more concerned to show that Jesus has fulfilled his mission, and has no interest in showing that Jesus ended his life citing Scripture. For him, the words 'It is finished' have more meaning.

This I shall call the 'moderate' view. It accepts that real events lie behind the Gospel stories but believes that they have been embellished as each Gospel writer adapts the tradition to meet his readers' needs. Thus Mark is known as the 'suffering Gospel' and seems to go out of its way to emphasize the suffering aspects of Jesus' ministry. John is at the other end of the spectrum, emphasizing that what looked like suffering was in reality Jesus' victory. Both are emphasizing those things their readers need to hear, but Mark's earlier date means that it is generally more reliable than John. The word 'generally' is important here. The earlier Gospels are generally more reliable than the later ones but that does not mean that everything in the latter is unreliable – it is possible that they sometimes had access to earlier sources that were unknown when the first Gospels were written.

There is a further feature of modern scholarship relevant to our study. Some 200 verses of Jesus' teaching are present in Matthew and Luke but not in Mark. These include such sayings as the Beatitudes ('Blessed are the meek . . .'), the Lord's prayer ('Our Father . . .') and certain parables, such as the marriage feast. Where did these sayings come from and are they earlier or later than Mark's Gospel? Most scholars believe they come from a sayings collection that is referred to as 'Q' (from the German *Quelle*, source) and is a decade earlier than Mark. Thus the traditional answer to the Synoptic problem is that Matthew and Luke both expanded Mark by incorporating additional teaching from Q and material that was known only to them (designated 'M' and 'L'). The 'moderate' view of Gospel study is that we can have some confidence in sayings found in Mark and Q but need to exercise caution with material found only in Mark or Luke (M and L), especially if it appears to serve the main emphases of these Gospels.

Before we embark on our study there is a third group of scholars that I will call 'minimalist'. By and large they agree with the analysis presented above but do not regard Mark as an accurate record of what Jesus said and did, which has implications for the accuracy of Matthew and Luke. Their reasons go back to a book by William Wrede, a famous German scholar active at the very beginning of the twentieth century.[5] He challenged the consensus view that Mark's abrupt and candid style was indicative of eyewitness testimony by showing that Mark is pursuing a theological agenda just as much as the other Gospels. For example, it was often said that stories that end with the disciples misunderstanding Jesus would hardly have been invented by the early Church. But Wrede suggested that Mark goes out of his way to portray Jesus as misunderstood, in order to explain the discrepancy between what the first disciples believed and what the later Church was proclaiming. For example, in Mark 8 the disciples are completely baffled as to how Jesus can feed a crowd of 4,000 with a few loaves and fishes, but not long before this – Mark 6 – they had seen Jesus feed a crowd of 5,000. Their lack of understanding is incomprehensible.

One of the key positions of modern 'minimalists' is that Jesus did not predict the future destruction of the world and his own return to earth. This has commonly been taught in churches ('he will come again to judge the living and the dead') and appears to be the teaching of the Synoptic Gospels – see Table I.2.

The key argument for the authenticity of these 'apocalyptic' sayings is that the end of the world did not come within a generation and Jesus has still not returned. Who then would have invented sayings that in the 70s and 80s (Matthew and Luke), if not in the 60s (Mark), would have been problematic? It was the argument of Albert Schweitzer[6] that Jesus believed that the end was nigh and that this is what gave the urgency to his preaching (repent while there is still time). The fact that it did not happen is a tremendous testimony to the accuracy of the scribes, who transmitted these sayings even though they knew they had not come true.

Scholars such as John Dominic Crossan argue differently. They believe that it was the furore surrounding the claim that Jesus had come back to life that led the early Church into thinking that the world was about to end. We know from texts like 1 Thessalonians 4.13–18 and 1 Corinthians 7.25–31 that this was Paul's belief in the early 50s, and so by the time Mark came to be written (late 60s) it was commonly thought that Jesus must have prophesied such things. Crossan thinks it is possible to reconstruct an early layer of wisdom traditions (mainly from Q but also the *Gospel of Thomas*) that represent Jesus' original teaching, with the apocalyptic layer coming later. We will discuss the complexities of this theory in Chapter 5, but it should now be clear why I call it 'minimalist'. Crossan believes that only a small proportion of the Gospel sayings go back

Table I.2

Matthew 24.29–31, 34	*Mark 13.24–27, 30*	*Luke 21.25–28, 32*
Immediately after the suffering of those days the sun will be darkened, and the moon will not give its light; the stars will fall from heaven, and the powers of heaven will be shaken. Then the sign of the Son of Man will appear in heaven, and then all the tribes of the earth will mourn, and they will see 'the Son of Man coming on the clouds of heaven' with power and great glory. And he will send out his angels with a loud trumpet call, and they will gather his elect from the four winds, from one end of heaven to the other . . .	But in those days, after that suffering, the sun will be darkened, and the moon will not give its light, and the stars will be falling from heaven, and the powers in the heavens will be shaken. Then they will see 'the Son of Man coming in clouds' with great power and glory. Then he will send out the angels, and gather his elect from the four winds, from the ends of the earth to the ends of heaven . . .	There will be signs in the sun, the moon, and the stars, and on the earth distress among nations confused by the roaring of the sea and the waves. People will faint from fear and foreboding of what is coming upon the world, for the powers of the heavens will be shaken. Then they will see 'the Son of Man coming in a cloud' with power and great glory. Now when these things begin to take place, stand up and raise your heads, because your redemption is drawing near . . .
Truly I tell you, this generation will not pass away until all these things have taken place.	*Truly I tell you, this generation will not pass away until all these things have taken place.*	*Truly I tell you, this generation will not pass away until all things have taken place.*

to Jesus, and interestingly for our purpose, this rarely involves Jesus' use of Scripture. Others would counter that a Jewish teacher such as Jesus almost certainly discussed and debated the meaning of Scripture, hence Crossan's portrait is fundamentally flawed.

Plan of the book

We will thus begin our study with a chapter on how Mark portrays Jesus' use of Scripture, followed by chapters on Matthew and Luke. We will be particularly interested in the sayings found in Matthew and Luke that the majority of scholars assign to Q, since this hypothetical source is usually dated a decade or so earlier than Mark. Our chapter on John is of interest in that John represents a very different tradition from the Synoptic Gospels, but only those of a maximalist position will use it to reconstruct Jesus' own use of Scripture. That is not to say that it is devoid of any historical traditions, as scholars such as John Robinson and Charles Dodd have shown, but they are generally embedded in discourses that reflect the theology of a later period.[7]

Having surveyed the material contained in the four Gospels, we then turn our attention to how this can be used to reconstruct Jesus' own use of Scripture. Since there is no consensus on how this should be done, we will group a number of scholars together under the three headings – minimalist, moderate and maximalist – mentioned above. This has the advantage of showing how the evidence can be construed when adopting different presuppositions, which will help readers decide for themselves which reconstruction they find the most convincing.

The question of Q

The main reason that scholars think Matthew and Luke used Q to expand the narrative outline of Mark is that there is often close agreement in the wording of a saying, even though it appears in a different context. This suggests that they were both copying from a text – the agreements sometimes involve unusual words or expressions – but each used it in his own way. Q would thus need to have existed for some time for it to be regarded as authoritative by both Matthew and Luke; hence a date in the 50s is proposed. It should be pointed out, however, that some scholars do not accept the existence of Q and believe that Matthew used a variety of sources and traditions to expand Mark, and that Luke obtained this material directly from Matthew. If this is the case, then Matthew is our only independent witness to this material, which means it could date from anytime between the 50s and 70s.[8]

1

Jesus and Scripture according to Mark's Gospel

Introduction

Mark is the shortest of the four Gospels (16 chapters), and moves rapidly from a ministry of teaching, healing and exorcism in Galilee (Mark 1—10) to the final week (the Passion) in Jerusalem (Mark 11—16). According to the best manuscripts, the Gospel ends with the story of the empty tomb (Mark 16.1–8) and does not record any resurrection stories. It used to be thought that Mark's original ending had been lost and that later scribes did their best to fill the gap (see the shorter and longer endings printed separately in the NRSV). But most scholars today believe that Mark deliberately ended his Gospel in an abrupt manner in order to stress the importance of the crucifixion. It corresponds with the abrupt beginning, where the story begins with Jesus' baptism and temptation and records the threat to his life as early as Mark 3.6.

There are about 25 quotations from the Old Testament in Mark's Gospel, of which some 22 are on the lips of Jesus. They are drawn from the law (10), the prophets (7) and the psalms (5). Since Mark is writing in Greek to a Greek-speaking audience, it is to be expected that the quotations would follow the LXX, which is generally the case. It is possible that Mark is responsible for this, but most scholars think that the translation of Jesus' sayings from Aramaic to Greek had happened long before Mark wrote his Gospel. The Gospel is usually dated between 65 and 69 CE, largely because Mark 13.14–23 seems to envisage a period just before the destruction of Jerusalem by the Roman armies (c. 70 CE). We will begin with Mark's view of Jesus' attitude to the law.

Jesus and the law

In the debate about hand washing in Mark 7 ('Why do your disciples not live according to the tradition of the elders, but eat with defiled hands?' – v. 5), Jesus criticizes their adherence to tradition because it involves 'abandoning' (v. 8) or 'rejecting' (v. 9) the commandment of God. He then cites the example of 'Corban', a law whereby a portion of one's goods can be dedicated to God and is therefore no longer available for mundane use, even if that means hardship for one's parents. This time Jesus accuses them of 'making void the word of God through your tradition' (v. 13), specifically citing the commandment to 'Honour your father and your mother' (v. 10). Thus Jesus is clearly portrayed as one who upholds the law and is hostile to 'traditions' (*halaka*) that undermine it.

This episode is followed by a discussion of what defiles a person, where Jesus says that 'there is nothing outside of a person that by going in can defile, but the things that come out are what defile' (v. 18). It is elaborated in verse 20 that the things in question are 'evil intentions' and that they come from the heart. There then follows a list of sins – drawn from the commandments (theft, murder, adultery) and other traditions (fornication, avarice, wickedness, deceit, licentiousness, envy, slander, pride, folly) – that come from the heart and defile. Thus in this episode Jesus upholds the law in the face of the human inclination to transgress it.

However, it is Mark's comment in the middle of this episode that has attracted attention. In verse 18, Jesus offers a rationale for why one is not defiled by what is outside: 'it enters, not the heart but the stomach, and goes out into the sewer'. This is then followed by a comment from Mark that literally translated means 'cleansing all foods' (NRSV: 'Thus he declared all foods clean'). It is not presented as words of Jesus, rather Mark's deduction from the aphorism. Thus we have a major difficulty with Mark's understanding of Jesus and the law. On the one hand, the episodes of Mark 7 strongly assert that Jesus upholds the law against Pharisaic tradition and the inclinations of the human heart. On the other hand, Mark thinks that Jesus' aphorism that 'there is nothing outside a person that by going in can defile' implies that all foods are clean, effectively abrogating a major section of the law and the principle – the distinction between clean and unclean – on which it is based.

A similar ambiguity occurs with the way Mark presents Jesus' view of the Sabbath. On the one hand, it is evidently Jesus' custom to be in the synagogue on the Sabbath (Mark 3.1; 6.2), and he undoubtedly upholds the Ten Commandments (Mark 10.19), even though the

Sabbath is not explicitly mentioned in his summary. But Mark 2.1—3.6 collect together a series of controversy stories, two of which focus on what can or cannot be done on the Sabbath. In Mark 2.23–28 the Pharisees object that Jesus' disciples are plucking grain as they make their way through the grain fields. Jesus replies by citing a story from 1 Samuel 21.1–6, where David entered the house of God and ate the consecrated bread, along with his companions. Jesus acknowledges that what David did was 'unlawful' but ends with the saying: 'The sabbath was made for humankind, and not humankind for the sabbath; so the Son of Man is lord even of the sabbath' (Mark 2.28). This is open to at least three interpretations:

1 Jesus has the authority to *break* the Sabbath, as his royal predecessor did.
2 Jesus has the authority to temporarily *suspend* the Sabbath because of the disciples' hunger, as with David and his companions.
3 Jesus has the authority to *declare* that the disciples' actions do not constitute a break with the Sabbath, contrary to Pharisaic tradition that regarded 'plucking grain' as a form of work (see Appendix 2).

Before trying to answer this we will consider the second controversy story (Mark 3.1–6) – the healing of the man with the withered hand. It is a Sabbath, and Jesus is in the synagogue along with the sick man. In this instance there is no verbal accusation by the Pharisees, but Mark tells us that Jesus knew they were watching him, 'to see whether he would cure him on the sabbath, so that they might accuse him' (v. 2). Jesus takes the argument to them by asking: 'Is it lawful to do good or to do harm on the sabbath, to save life or to kill?' (v. 4). Since he then proceeds to heal the man, it is clear that Jesus does not regard his healing activity as breaking the Sabbath, contrary to the view of the Pharisees. Indeed, Mark tells us that the Pharisees immediately went out to conspire with the Herodians to have Jesus put to death (v. 6). Mark clearly intends this to be ironic: the Pharisees complain that Jesus is breaking the commandments while they themselves are engaged in a plot to have someone murdered.

Thus it would appear that Mark does not regard Jesus as breaking the Sabbath, although his interpretation of it is clearly at loggerheads with Pharisaic tradition. Whether Mark is correct in this will be discussed in Chapters 5–7, but two points are worth mentioning here.

First, if this healing corresponds to what actually happened, the Pharisees would surely have pointed out that the man's life was not at risk. If Jesus truly respected the Sabbath, why did he not wait until the following day to heal him? Second, if Jesus defended the disciples' plucking of grain on the Sabbath by reference to David eating the consecrated bread, they would surely have pointed out that in that story there is no mention of it being on a Sabbath (1 Sam. 21.1–6). What is clear is that *Mark* thinks that Jesus upheld the spirit of the Sabbath against Pharisaic traditions.

We thus return to the question of the food laws. Is it likely that Mark thinks that Jesus castigated the Pharisees for 'abandoning', 'rejecting' or 'making void' God's commandments for the sake of their traditions, only to abrogate the food laws on the basis of an aphorism about what defiles a person? If we remember that the discussion began over the issue of Pharisaic hand-washing rituals (Mark 7.1–5), it could be argued that Mark's conclusion – 'cleansing all foods' – has nothing to do with the law's distinction between clean and unclean food. It is simply asserting that food does not become defiled by breaking the detailed hand-washing rituals of the Pharisees. The status of food that the law regards as unclean is simply not in view. Indeed, although Jesus is accused of eating with tax collectors and sinners (Mark 2.16), he is never accused of eating anything unclean, which concurs with Peter's protestation in Acts 10.14 that never in his life – thus including his time with Jesus – has he ever eaten anything unclean. Therefore while the question of Mark's attitude to the law continues to be a matter of debate,[1] most scholars think that Jesus kept the Jewish food laws and at no time spoke against them.

This appears to be confirmed by a number of other texts where Jesus is seen to uphold the authority of the law. For example, having healed the man suffering from leprosy in Mark 1.42, he tells him to 'go, show yourself to the priest, and offer for your cleansing what Moses commanded, as a testimony to them' (Mark 1.44). When the young ruler asks what he has to do to inherit eternal life, Jesus directs him to the commandments (Mark 10.19). The fact that Jesus adds the requirement to sell his possessions and give to the poor is hardly a criticism of the commandments. When the Sadducees seek to trap him with a concocted story about a woman forced to marry seven brothers after each dies (based on the levirate law of Deuteronomy

25.5), he replies: 'Is not this the reason you are wrong, that you know neither the scriptures nor the power of God?' (Mark 12.24). He then argues from the book of Exodus that because God said 'I am the God of Abraham, the God of Isaac, and the God of Jacob' (Exod. 3.15), the dead must be raised. One might have expected a quotation from one of the texts in the Old Testament that speak of resurrection, such as Daniel 12.1–2, but this is probably to be explained by the fact that the Sadducees regarded the prophets as secondary to the law. According to John Meier, the logic of Jesus' reply is this:

1 Throughout Scripture, God refers to himself as the God of Abraham, Isaac and Jacob.
2 Scripture also says that God is a God of the living, not the defiling, unclean dead.
3 Therefore Abraham, Isaac and Jacob must be 'alive' with God (now or in the future).[2]

However, there are two further stories that might challenge this view. The first is the discussion about divorce in Mark 10.2–9. The Pharisees ask Jesus whether it is lawful for a man to divorce his wife. Jewish sources suggest that this was a hotly debated subject, some arguing that divorce was possible for almost any reason (the school of Hillel), others taking a more rigorous line and insisting that the reason had to be something serious, such as adultery (the school of Shammai). Jesus responds by asking them what Moses commanded, and they reply by quoting words from Deuteronomy 24.1–4 ('Moses allowed a man to write a certificate of dismissal and to divorce her'), the only passage in the law to mention divorce. However, this is evidently not Jesus' position, for he says that this was written 'because of your hardness of heart', and goes on to quote Genesis 1.27 and 2.24, that marriage is about two people becoming one flesh. Although these texts do not mention divorce, Jesus deduces that 'one flesh' implies 'no divorce', and so goes beyond even the rigorous position of Shammai: 'Whoever divorces his wife and marries another commits adultery against her; and if she divorces her husband and marries another, she commits adultery' (Mark 10.11–12).

Although one could argue that Jesus is not contradicting the law (Deuteronomy 24 permits divorce but does not command it), he is clearly giving the Genesis texts priority over the Deuteronomy text. Indeed, John Meier says that Jesus' position on divorce is nothing short of astounding: 'Jesus presumes to teach that what the Law permits and regulates is actually the sin of adultery.'[3] In other words, the Jewish man who conscientiously follows the Torah's rules for divorce and remarriage is in fact guilty of breaking one of the Ten Commandments. According to Meier, this is much more than entering the debate about permissible grounds for divorce. On the other hand, Jesus is not the first to give priority to the Genesis text. We find the same argument in a text from the Dead Sea Scrolls, though it is unclear whether it is condemning polygamy or divorce:[4]

> The 'builders of the wall' [possibly Pharisees] ... who have followed after 'Precept '– 'Precept' ... shall be caught in fornication twice by taking a second wife while the first is alive, whereas the principle of creation is, *Male and female created He them* ...   (CD 4.20–21)

Our second example is where Jesus is asked, 'Which commandment is the first of all?' (Mark 12.28). He replies by affirming the traditional confession (known as the *Shema*): 'Hear, O Israel: the Lord our God, the Lord is one; you shall love the Lord your God with all your heart, and with all your soul, and with all your mind, and with all your strength' (Mark 12.29–30). However, he then goes beyond the scribe's question by asserting: 'The second is this, "You shall love your neighbour as yourself"' (Mark 12.31), adding that there is 'no other commandment [singular] greater than these'.

Combining the commandments to love God and neighbour was not unique to Jesus. In a work entitled *The Testaments of the Twelve Patriarchs*, we read in the *Testament of Issachar*, 'love the Lord and your neighbour' (*T. Iss.* 5.2), and in the *Testament of Dan*, 'love the Lord and one another with a true heart' (*T. Dan* 5.3). However, there do not appear to be any parallels to citing them as the first and second commandments, although Philo and Josephus both think of the Ten Commandments as pertaining to God (first five) and neighbour (second five). It would appear to cohere with Mark's view that Jesus upheld the law but was antagonistic towards Pharisaic traditions that (in his view) diverted it from its humanitarian intentions. Thus Jesus is against using the 'permission' to divorce in Deuteronomy 24 as a path to adultery, or the dedication of goods to God (Corban) to avoid obligation to one's parents. In Jesus' view (as portrayed by Mark), such traditions do not 'uphold' the law, as the Pharisees claim, but undermine its true intent.

However, there are two further features of this story that require comment. The first is technical, and it is that Jesus cites four faculties (heart, soul, mind, strength), whereas Deuteronomy 6.5 only has three (heart, soul, might). It is inconceivable that Mark was not aware of this and indeed he has the scribe repeat Jesus' answer with just three ('You are right, Teacher; you have truly said that "he is one, and besides him there is no other"; and "to love him with all the heart, and with all the understanding, and with all the strength"'). We might compare this with Jesus' citation of the Ten Commandments in Mark 10.19, where honouring parents comes *after* murder, adultery, theft and false witness, and instead of the command not to covet we have the command not to defraud. It was evidently not Mark's purpose to show that upholding the law is dependent on citing its precise wording.

Second, Mark has the scribe make a deduction from Jesus' reply ('this is much more important than all whole burnt-offerings and sacrifices'), which gains Jesus' approval ('When Jesus saw that he answered wisely'). As with his parenthetical comment about 'cleansing all foods', this looks like Mark's comment to make the point that moral laws are more important than ritual laws. It does not necessarily represent Jesus' view and as we shall see in the next chapter, it does not appear in Matthew's version of the story. Bill Loader thinks that Mark is deliberately contrasting 'heart religion' with 'cultic observance' for the benefit of his Gentile readers.[5] This might be so, though it is worth noting that the scribe speaks of 'more important' (*perisotteron*) rather than replacement, and in this he is no different from many of Israel's prophets (Isa. 1.11; Hos. 6.6). In conclusion, Mark presents Jesus as a law-abiding Jew who was at odds with any who would use 'tradition', or even the law itself, as a means of avoiding what he considered to be the true intent of the law.

Jesus and the prophets

Mark opens his Gospel with either a statement or title ('The beginning of the good news of Jesus Christ, the Son of God'), followed by a composite quotation of Malachi 3.1/Exodus 23.20 ('See, I am sending my messenger ahead of you, who will prepare your way') and Isaiah 40.3 ('the voice of one crying out in the wilderness: "Prepare the way of the Lord, make his paths straight"'). According to the best manuscripts, the composite quotation is introduced by the words 'As it is written in the prophet Isaiah', which later manuscripts changed to 'in the prophets' (so KJV) to conform to the composite quotation. However, many scholars believe that the specific reference to Isaiah is significant, indicating not only that the messenger (John the Baptist) was prophesied in Scripture but that the 'beginning of the good news of Jesus Christ' was written in Isaiah. We will thus begin this section with an examination of Jesus' use of Isaiah.

The first clear reference to Isaiah comes in Mark 4.12, where Jesus answers the disciples' question about the meaning of parables by saying: 'To you has been given the secret of the kingdom of God, but for those outside, everything comes in parables; in order that "they may indeed *look*, but not *perceive*, and may indeed *listen*, but *not understand*; so that they may not *turn* again and be *forgiven*."' The reference is somewhat controversial since it appears to be saying that Jesus deliberately spoke in parables so that outsiders would not be able to comprehend and be forgiven. The words come from Isaiah's call-vision, where he is not only told that Israel will reject his message but that this rejection is part of God's purposes:

> Go and say to this people: 'Keep *listening*, but do *not comprehend*; keep *looking*, but do *not understand*.' Make the mind of this people dull, and stop their ears, and shut their eyes, so that they may not look with their eyes, and listen with their ears, and comprehend with their minds, and *turn* and *be healed*.   (Isa. 6.9–10)

Joachim Jeremias famously argued that the difficulty arose through mistranslation. The Greek word *parabole* translates the Hebrew *mashal*, which can mean riddle, puzzle, dark saying or oracle. He concluded that what Jesus meant was something like 'for those outside, it all sounds like riddles', but when this was translated into Greek it became 'for those outside, everything comes in parables'. Mark then added to the confusion by placing it in the middle of his parables chapter, suggesting that the purpose of the parables was to hide rather than to reveal. Jeremias thought that this explanation was confirmed by the fact that elsewhere in Mark, the parables are clearly intended to be understood by the hearers (Mark 12.12).[6]

Bill Telford disagrees. He does not think this is a case of Mark misunderstanding the saying but of deliberate reinterpretation. Whatever Jesus may have meant by comparing the dull response to his teaching with Isaiah's commission, Mark thinks that 'the parables were *meant* to harden Jewish hearts, *meant* to make them misunderstand, *meant* to conceal . . . for history is governed by God's purposes which cannot be thwarted.'[7] As we shall see in the following chapter, Matthew uses a different Greek word to connect the Isaiah citation with Jesus' saying, with the effect that the blindness is a 'result' (*hoste*) of the parables, but not their purpose (*hina*).

It is of interest that later in Mark, the accusation of blindness, based on Isaiah 6.9–10, is also aimed at the disciples. They are on a boat journey with Jesus and realize that they have forgotten to bring enough bread (Mark 8.14). Thus when Jesus warns them against the 'yeast of the Pharisees', they assume that he is having a dig at them for forgetting the bread. This calls forth the following accusation: 'Why are you talking about having no bread? Do you still not perceive or understand? Are your hearts hardened? Do you have eyes, and fail to see? Do you have ears, and fail to hear?' Taken on its own, this could be an allusion to Jeremiah 5.21 or even Ezekiel 12.2, but it is almost certain that Mark intends his readers to connect this with the parable purpose of Mark 4.12. If outsiders cannot understand the kingdom because they have eyes that cannot see and ears that cannot hear, then the same is true of the disciples, raising a key question for Mark's Gospel: Did anyone believe in his message?

The second explicit reference to Isaiah is found in the controversy over hand washing (Mark 7.1–23), Jesus' response (before the aphorism about what defiles – see p. 14) is to say that 'Isaiah prophesied rightly about you hypocrites' and then to quote words from Isaiah 29.13: 'This people honours me with their lips, but their hearts are far from me; in vain do they worship me, teaching human precepts as doctrines.' This is then illustrated by the law of Corban, where they are said to put their 'traditions', which are therefore being equated with the 'human precepts' of the quotation, before the commandment of God. Mark follows the LXX in referring to 'teaching human precepts as doctrines', whereas the Hebrew text is more specific, stating that it is their *worship* which is governed by human precepts. Since the LXX rendering undoubtedly facilitates the application to the Pharisees, who are accused of using their traditions to avoid upholding the commandments, many scholars are sceptical that this goes back to Jesus. But it is clearly Mark's view that Jesus applied Isaiah 29.13 to the hypocrisy of the Pharisees.

The Pharisees

One of the reasons that some scholars challenge the reliability of Mark's Gospel is that its picture of the Pharisees is so different from what is found in Jewish sources. Thus, contrary to the Sadducees, who focused on the priesthood, and the Qumran community, who focused on monastic observance, the Pharisees believed that the law could be fulfilled in daily life. This sometimes meant adopting 'traditions' that went beyond the law, but there is no evidence that they were hostile to less observant Jews. Neither is there evidence that they would have opposed healing on the Sabbath or would have disagreed with Jesus that the commandment to honour parents takes priority over the tradition of Corban. Noting that Jewish debate often used hyperbole (exaggeration) and rhetoric (caricature), Sanders concludes that none of the disputes found in the Gospels falls outside the parameters of ordinary Jewish debate (see Appendix 2).[8]

The third explicit reference comes in the so-called cleansing of the temple incident, where Jesus issues the following accusation on God's behalf: 'Is it not written, "My house shall be called a house of prayer for all the nations"? But you have made it a den of robbers' (Mark 11.17). The words come from Isaiah 56.7, with the phrase 'den of robbers' from Jeremiah 7.11. The precise nature of the accusation is not clear. If Mark has the context of Isaiah 56.7 in mind, then the emphasis is on inclusion ('for the nations'). Jesus is condemning the commercial activity of the temple courts because it excludes Gentiles. It is of interest that the way Isaiah 56.7 expresses this is to say of the 'foreigners' and 'eunuchs' that 'their burnt-offerings and their sacrifices will be accepted on my altar' – further evidence that Mark does not think that Jesus was against ritual in itself. On the other hand, Mark has combined Isaiah 56.7 with words from Jeremiah 7.11 ('den of robbers'), which might suggest that *corruption* rather than exclusion is the focus of his protest. If this is the case, then the emphasis of the Isaiah quotation falls on the words 'house of prayer', in contrast to the 'den of robbers' that it has become.

Most scholars recognize a fourth reference to Isaiah in the parable of the vineyard (Mark 12.1–11). Some scholars think that this parable began life as a protest against absentee landlords, but in Mark's version it is clearly intended to be a reference to the song of the vineyard in Isaiah 5. This is seen by the following parallels:

1 the construction details specifically mention digging a wine vat and erecting a watchtower (Isa. 5.2/Mark 12.1);
2 the vineyard fails to return fruit to its owner (Isa. 5.4/Mark 12.3);
3 the people of the vineyard turn to murderous behaviour (Isa. 5.7/ Mark 12.5);
4 they incur destruction by the owner (Isa. 5.5/Mark 12.9).

What is different about Jesus' parable is that a series of emissaries are sent by the owner/landlord before the vineyard is destroyed. This is almost certainly a reference to the prophets (2 Kings 9.7; Jer. 7.25; Ezek. 38.17), so Jesus is portrayed as *extending* the allegory to cover the whole period of Israel's relationship with God.

What stands out from these four explicit references to Isaiah discussed in the foregoing paragraphs is that they are all concerned with Jesus' opponents: Isaiah 6.9–10 is applied to their blindness; Isaiah 29.13 to their hypocrisy; Isaiah 56.7 to either their exclusivity or corruption; and Isaiah 5 to their unfruitfulness and violence. As we shall see in Chapters 5–7, one of the major questions facing the reconstruction of Jesus' use of Scripture is whether such quotations reflect later disputes between Church and Synagogue rather than between Jesus and his fellow Jews. What is clear is that Mark portrays Jesus as seeing in Isaiah a series of prophecies concerning those who are opposing him. This raises the question of how he viewed himself, the recipient of this opposition, and the most likely answer is that he viewed himself as the one who suffers in Isaiah 40—55.

The strongest evidence for this comes in Mark 10.45, where Jesus (under the epithet of 'the Son of Man') says that he 'came not to be served but to serve, and to give his life a ransom for many'. When this is combined with the words spoken at the last supper in Mark 14.24 ('This is my blood of the covenant, which is poured out for many'), there is an obvious parallel with Isaiah 53.11–12:

> The righteous one, my *servant, shall make many righteous,* and he shall bear their iniquities. Therefore I will allot him a portion with the great, and he shall divide the spoil with the strong; because he *poured out*

himself to death, and was numbered with the transgressors; yet he
bore the sin of *many*, and made intercession for the transgressors.

(Isa. 53.11–12)

Morna Hooker famously objected to such an identification, pointing
out that Mark has managed to use a different Greek word from what
is in the LXX for all of the key terms: 'service/servant'; 'ransom'; 'poured
out'.[9] Although it could be argued that Jesus originally spoke these
sayings in Aramaic, so that differences from the LXX are irrelevant,
it does raise the question of how Mark thought his readers, who are
unlikely to have known much Aramaic, would have made the identification. Put another way, if Mark intended his readers to grasp the
fact that Jesus saw himself as the suffering servant of Isaiah 53, why
did he not make this more explicit, either with an explicit quotation
or at least some use of the key vocabulary from that chapter?

Those who believe that Mark does intend such an identification
point to the opening quotation, which could suggest that the events
that are to follow are not just in accord with Isaiah 40.3 but also the
material that it introduces, namely Isaiah 40—55. There is also the
suggestion that the words at Jesus' baptism in Mark 1.11 ('You are
my Son, the Beloved; with you I am well pleased') reflect the language
of the servant in Isaiah 42.1a ('Here is my servant, whom I uphold,
my chosen, in whom my soul delights'), while the descent of the
Spirit accords with Isaiah 42.1b ('I have put my spirit upon him').
In response, one could say that if Mark intended the quotation of
Isaiah 40.3 to indicate that Jesus fulfils the role of the servant in Isaiah
40—55, why does he complicate this by making it a composite quotation, with words from Malachi 3.1/Exodus 23.20 coming first? And
if Mark intends the words at the baptism to suggest the servant of
Isaiah 42.1, why does he point his readers to Psalm 2.7 ('You are my
son'), where the king is being addressed? At best, one would have to
say that Mark's presentation leaves the issue of whether Jesus thought
of himself as the servant of Isaiah 40—55 ambiguous.

After the last supper, Jesus leads the disciples to the Mount of
Olives and predicts their desertion (Mark 14.27), quoting words from
Zechariah 13.7 in the form: 'I will strike the shepherd, and the sheep
will be scattered'. In the original, a sword is addressed ('Awake, O
sword, against my shepherd . . . Strike the shepherd'), but Mark ig-
nores this and assumes that it is God who does the striking. It does

not seem a very appropriate reference since God appears to be angry with both the shepherd and the sheep, but the clue might come in what follows. Zechariah says that two-thirds of the people will perish but a third will be refined by fire so that they will 'call on my name, and I will answer them' (Zech. 13.9). Some have argued that this is the point of the quotation – it predicts the desertion and return to faith of the disciples, and we know from the rest of the New Testament that this is in fact what happened (except for Judas). However, this is not the part of Zechariah that is quoted, so it must be assumed that Mark's readers would readily know what comes next. As with our discussion of Jesus and the Servant, it does not appear to be Mark's purpose to make the identification with Zechariah's stricken shepherd explicit.

Finally, we will consider the apocalyptic language that occurs in Mark 13. The chapter begins with the disciples' admiration of the temple and Jesus' response that it will be destroyed ('Not one stone will be left here upon another; all will be thrown down'). He then utters a prophecy, similar in style to the Old Testament prophets, which begins with earthly woes (wars, earthquakes, famines) and leads on to what appears to be the end of the world:

> But in those days, after that suffering, the sun will be darkened, and the moon will not give its light, and the stars will be falling from heaven, and the powers in the heavens will be shaken. Then they will see 'the Son of Man coming in clouds' with great power and glory. Then he will send out the angels, and gather his elect from the four winds, from the ends of the earth to the ends of heaven.
>
> (Mark 13.24–26)

As is common in the apocalyptic style, phrases from different Scriptures are fused together to give a powerful and evocative warning of future judgement. The reference to sun and moon draws on Isaiah 13.10 and Joel 2.10 (also 3.4; 4.15). Stars falling from heaven echoes Isaiah 34.4, while the gathering of the elect suggests Zechariah 2.6. But most attention has focused on the reference to 'the Son of Man coming in clouds', which reflects the figure in Daniel's dream: 'I saw in the night visions, and behold, with the clouds of heaven there came one like a son of man, and he came to the Ancient of Days and was presented before him' (Dan. 7.13 rsv). Most of the discussion has centred on the authenticity of the saying, since the words translated

25

'son of man' would simply mean 'human' or 'mortal' when spoken in Aramaic (hence the NRSV translation, 'I saw one like a human being'); they would not have been understood as a title ('*the* Son of Man'). This is an important issue, also affecting whether Jesus' reply in Mark 2.28 means that 'humanity' is lord of the Sabbath (because the Sabbath was made for humanity, not humanity for the Sabbath) or specifically that Jesus, as *the* Son of Man, is lord of the Sabbath. At present, we will confine ourselves to Mark's probable meaning.

Daniel is referring to a human-like figure (as opposed to the four beasts of Dan. 7.1–8) who comes to God and receives 'dominion and glory and kingship, that all peoples, nations, and languages should serve him. His dominion is an everlasting dominion that shall not pass away, and his kingship is one that shall never be destroyed' (Dan. 7.14). As this stands, it sounds like a prophecy of the messiah's reign, but when Daniel asks about the meaning of the visions, he is told that the four beasts represent four kings (usually understood to be Babylon, Persia, Greece and Rome), while it is the 'holy ones of the Most High' who will receive the everlasting kingdom. Either the 'son of man' is a symbol for God's people or it combines both individual and corporate traits (as perhaps Isaiah's 'servant' does). How then does Mark understand Jesus' words?

The traditional view is that Mark thinks that Jesus is referring to his second coming, that is, his return to earth in judgement (Acts 1.11; 1 Thess. 4.14). The difficulty with this view is that Mark 13 says nothing about Jesus coming *to the earth*, and if the allusion to Daniel 7.13 is deliberate, then it evokes the image of a figure going *to God*, not coming *from God*. Consequently, other views have been suggested that take the allusion to Dan. 7.13 in a less literal sense. Daniel is referring to the replacement of evil kingdoms with God's perfect everlasting kingdom, and that is what the allusion is intended to evoke. Thus in answer to the disciples' question concerning the fate of the temple, Jesus responds by saying (in symbolic language) that the temple will be destroyed and replaced by an everlasting kingdom, that of the messiah and his people. If it is replied that the cosmic language of sun and moon not giving their light and stars falling from heaven is rather excessive for a description of the destruction of the temple, it has been argued that the texts referred to earthly calamities in their original contexts. Richard France puts it like this:

the apocalyptic language of these verses, drawn almost entirely from identifiable OT texts, relates, as did those texts in their own contexts, not to the collapse of the physical universe and the end of the world but to imminent and far-reaching political change, in the context of the predicted destruction of Jerusalem. On this view the 'coming of the Son of Man' is language not about an eschatological descent of Jesus to the earth but, as in the vision of Daniel from which it derives, about the vindication and enthronement of the Son of Man at the right hand of God, to receive and exercise supreme authority.[10]

There is a further allusion to Daniel 7.13 in Jesus' reply to the high priest at his trial (Mark 14.62). The high priest asks Jesus, 'Are you the Messiah, the Son of the Blessed One?' For the first time in Mark's Gospel, Jesus openly accepts the titles and replies: 'I am; and "you will see the Son of Man seated at the right hand of the Power", and "coming with the clouds of heaven."' The reference to being seated at God's right hand is probably an allusion to Psalm 110.1 ('Sit at my right hand until I make your enemies your footstool'), especially as this text is explicitly quoted in Mark 12.35–37. With typical Jewish reverence, the high priest avoids pronouncing the name of God by using a circumlocution ('Blessed One'), and Jesus does likewise ('the Power'). But what Jesus says next is offensive to the high priest and results in a charge of 'blasphemy' (Mark 14.64).

It begins with a prediction that they (the 'you' is plural) will see something, which later Christian theology has understood to be Jesus' second coming. This depends on taking the two phrases as sequential, so that Jesus 'sits' at God's right hand (for a time) and then 'comes' on the clouds (at the end of time). However, since the 'sitting' is clearly metaphorical and is not something that can be (visibly) seen, it is worth enquiring as to whether this is also true of the 'coming'. We have already noted that Daniel 7.13 is not referring to a 'coming' to earth but a 'coming' to God in order to receive a kingdom. Thus like Psalm 110.1, Daniel 7.13 is an enthronement oracle, where the recipient does not 'go' anywhere in a literal sense but receives power and authority.

Is this how Mark understood it? The high priest thinks that Jesus is worthy of death, but there will come a time when he (and those with him) will 'see' that God does not agree; far from it – they will 'see' that God has given Jesus a kingdom of power and authority. Mark may have thought this was fulfilled in the resurrection (Mark 9.1), the coming of the Spirit (Mark 13.11) or the destruction of the temple

(Mark 13.2). As we shall see later, this raises an interesting conundrum in terms of what Jesus might have meant. On the one hand, if Jesus was referring to one of these 'earthly' events, was the Church wrong to develop its view of a second coming of Jesus? On the other hand, if Jesus was thinking of a second coming (and the end of the world), then the high priest did not live to see it and Jesus was wrong.

Finally, although no explicit quotations are involved, there is an intriguing discussion that takes place after the story of Jesus' transfiguration. In that story Moses and Elijah appear on the mountain with Jesus (Mark 9.5), which prompts the disciple's question, 'Why do the scribes say that Elijah must come first?' (Mark 9.11). This is puzzling, since they have just seen Elijah, and Jesus' reply is equally puzzling:

> Elijah is indeed coming first to restore all things. How then is it written about the Son of Man, that he is to go through many sufferings and be treated with contempt? But I tell you that Elijah has come, and they did to him whatever they pleased, as it is written about him.
>
> (Mark 9.12–13)

Three things are difficult about Jesus' reply. First, he appears to endorse the scribal belief that Elijah is coming to restore all things (based on the reference to Elijah in Malachi 4.5 and the LXX's use of the word 'restore' in the next verse), but then states that Elijah has already come. The 'restoration' envisaged in Malachi 4.6 is the healing of relationships within Israel ('He will turn the hearts of parents to their children and the hearts of children to their parents'), but this has hardly been fulfilled. Second, the fate of the Son of Man and the fate of Elijah are said to be in accord with what is written, a formula that elsewhere means 'written in Scripture' (Mark 1.2; 7.6; 11.17). There is debate as to whether texts such as Isaiah 53 or Psalm 22 are in the background for the fate of the Son of Man (the actual phrase does not occur), but there are no texts or Jewish traditions that speak about a suffering Elijah. Third, the statement about the 'Son of Man' intrudes between the two Elijah sayings, making it difficult to see the underlying logic. That these are genuine difficulties rather than our modern desire for coherence can be seen by the fact that Matthew places the 'Son of Man' saying after the two Elijah sayings, and omits any reference to Scripture (Matt. 17.10–12).

Joel Marcus suggests that some of these difficulties are solved if we understand Jesus' first remark as, effectively, a question ('Does

Elijah restore all things?'), as the Greek would allow.[11] He believes it is an example of a common Jewish exegetical practice whereby difficulties in Scripture are resolved. In this case, the scribes think that Elijah's restoration will be something glorious, just as they think that the Messiah will come in power. Jesus responds by saying that Scripture (also) says that the 'Son of Man' will suffer, and deduces from this that the same must be true of his forerunner. Thus the second reference to what is written is not referring to a specific text but the exegetical procedure that has just been written by Mark.[12]

France finds this somewhat fanciful and suggests that Mark is not so much thinking about a specific verse but the Elijah stories in general, where he was 'driven by his faithfulness to God's commission into potentially fatal conflict with the royal house (1 Ki. 19:2–3, 10, 14)'.[13] The difference is that Herodias succeeded where Jezebel failed (equating Elijah with John the Baptist, Mark 6.17–29), which confirms to Jesus that this will be his fate also. Jesus is not therefore claiming that the restoration of Malachi 4.5 has been fulfilled, but directs the scribes to the stories about Elijah's conflict with the king. France calls this a 'typological' reading, meaning that certain people or events in Scripture parallel certain people and events in a later period.

Jesus and the writings

If the opening quotation from Isaiah 40.3 (and Malachi 3.1/Exodus 23.20) indicates the importance of Isaiah for understanding Mark's account of Jesus, the words at the baptism play a similar role for the psalms. According to Mark's account (Mark 1.10–11), the heavens are torn apart (*schizo*), the Spirit descends on him like a dove and a voice from heaven says to him 'You are my Son, the Beloved; with you I am well pleased.' This richly allusive phrase may draw on Genesis 22.2 (Isaac is called a 'beloved son'), Jeremiah 31.20 (Ephraim is called a 'beloved son') and Isaiah 42.1 (the servant in whom God delights), but it is Psalm 2.7 that is the principal text. This royal psalm addresses David as God's anointed ('You are my son; today I have begotten you'), and promises to make the nations his heritage and the ends of the earth his possession (Ps. 2.8). The words are repeated in the transfiguration story, where this time it is the disciples who are addressed: 'This is my Son, the Beloved; listen to him!' (Mark 9.7). The psalm was important in the early Church for establishing the 'sonship' of Jesus (Acts 13.33; Heb. 1.5; Rev. 12.5), and Mark no doubt expects his readers to remember it when they encounter the 'beloved son' in the parable of the vineyard.

However, contrary to the exalted claims of Psalm 2.8–9 (that the 'beloved son' will reign over the earth), the son in the parable is killed by the tenants (Mark 12.7). But this is not the end of the story, for Jesus goes on to quote words from Psalm 118.22–23: 'The stone that the builders rejected has become the cornerstone; this was the Lord's doing, and it is amazing in our eyes'. While some scholars believe this is a rather clumsy attempt to 'resurrect' the son in line with Christian doctrine, others point to the wordplay that exists between the Hebrew words for 'son' (*ben*) and 'stone' (*eben*) as a suitable rationale for the connection (which does not work in Greek as the words are *huios* and *lithos*). The quotation makes two points. First, the death/rejection of the son/stone becomes the cornerstone for a new building, which Mark undoubtedly understands as the Church. Second, the phrase 'this was the Lord's doing' confirms a point made in the Passion predictions (Mark 8.31; 9.31; 10.33) that Jesus' crucifixion was part of God's plan. How much of this goes back to Jesus will be discussed in Chapters 5–7.

Most of the disputes in Mark's Gospel begin with a challenge to Jesus, but in Mark 12.35–37 Jesus is portrayed as taking the initiative. While teaching in the temple he asks, 'How can the scribes say that the Messiah is the son of David?' He then quotes Psalm 110.1 as a riddle, for if David (by the Holy Spirit) calls him Lord, how can he be his son ('The Lord said to my Lord, "Sit at my right hand, until I put your enemies under your feet"')? The Hebrew text makes it clear that the first 'Lord' is God (YHWH), and in the light of the promise (subjection of enemies), God is speaking to his Messiah, whom David addresses as 'my Lord' (*adonai*). Later Christian thought will argue that the LXX – which uses *kyrios* for both YHWH and *adonai* here – refers to God the Father speaking to God the Son, but is this Mark's meaning? Joel Marcus thinks that Mark is wrestling with an ambiguity:

> Paradoxically . . . the Davidic image turns out to be both too trium-phalistic and not triumphant enough . . . It is not triumphant enough because Jesus is victor not only over his earthly enemies but also, as his entire earthly ministry reveals, over their supernatural masters . . .

That image, on the other hand, is too triumphant because the manner in which Jesus wins his definitive victory over his enemies is through his suffering and death.[14]

It has been a puzzle and sometimes a theological embarrassment that God's Messiah ends his life in Mark's Gospel with the cry 'My God, my God, why have you forsaken me?' (Mark 15.34). These are the opening words (after the title) of Psalm 22, and one suggestion is that Jesus was seeking to invoke the whole of the psalm, especially its more positive ending: 'For he did not despise or abhor the affliction of the afflicted; he did not hide his face from me, but heard when I cried to him . . . future generations will be told about the Lord, and proclaim his deliverance to a people yet unborn, saying that he has done it' (Ps. 22.24, 30–31). Certainly Mark appears to have the wider psalm in mind, for the dividing of Jesus' garments alludes to Psalm 22.18 ('they divide my clothes among themselves, and for my clothing they cast lots') and the mockery and wagging of heads alludes to Psalm 22.7 ('All who see me mock at me; they make mouths at me, they shake their heads'). However, these allusions merely confirm that Mark's focus is on the suffering of the psalmist, not the psalm's more positive conclusion. As France says, 'to read into these few tortured words an exegesis of the whole psalm is to turn upside down the effect which Mark has created by this powerful and enigmatic cry of agony'.[15] It thus appears that Mark understood Psalm 22.1 as a prophecy of the Messiah's suffering, just as he has portrayed Jesus' suffering as God's will throughout his Gospel.[16]

The criterion of embarrassment

In this chapter we have seen several examples of where Jesus' words are not easy to reconcile with later Christian beliefs and practices. For example, Mark 4.10–12 states that Jesus spoke in parables so that his hearers could not perceive his meaning. This is very different from the idea that Jesus spoke in parables in order to communicate to a wide audience. In the story of the man enquiring about eternal life Jesus says 'Why do you call me good? No one is good but God alone' (Mark 10.18). In Mark 10.11 Jesus forbids divorce on any grounds, a teaching that Paul finds difficult to apply in the case of a Christian married to a non-Christian (1 Cor. 7.12–16). And as we have just discussed, it is surprising that God's faithful servant ends his life by crying out 'My God, my God, why have you forsaken me?' (Mark 15.32), especially as the first Christian martyr (Stephen) seems far more composed (Acts 7.54–56). *The criterion of embarrassment* states that it is very unlikely that the early Church would invent sayings that contradict or otherwise differ from its own beliefs and practices. It is more likely that they have been included because the Gospel writers (or their sources) knew that Jesus had said them, even though they present the Church with certain difficulties.

Conclusion

Mark's Gospel is often thought of as the 'enigmatic Gospel', and this also applies to his portrayal of Jesus' use of Scripture. Thus he presents Jesus as strongly upholding the law against Pharisaic 'traditions', while almost going out of his way to provoke them concerning what can and cannot be done on the Sabbath. He refers to the Scriptures as the 'word of God' but suggests that the 'one flesh' view of marriage in Genesis 2 takes priority over the permission to divorce in Deuteronomy 24, which is said to be a concession by Moses. Isaiah is clearly an important text to Jesus, but the explicit quotations are not used to elucidate who he is and what he has come to do, rather to accuse his opponents of blindness, hypocrisy and self-interest. The psalms are also important to Jesus, and Mark probably thinks that the voice at the baptism and transfiguration ('You are my son') were significant for Jesus' own self-understanding. However, contrary to the victory message of Psalm 2, the son in the parable of the vineyard is killed and Jesus ends his life by identifying with David's suffering in Psalm 22, which if understood as prophecy becomes the suffering of the Messiah. The only explicit quotation that makes the point that suffering will not have the final word is Psalm 118.23, quoted at the end of the parable of the vineyard. The son in the parable is killed but the psalm envisages the son/stone becoming the cornerstone of a new building, which Mark undoubtedly understands as the Church. It remains a matter of debate as to why the allusions to Isaiah 53 are so tentative when quotations from this chapter would have brought some coherence to Mark's 'victory through suffering' theme. Perhaps coherence, in the sense of rational explanation, was not what Mark was trying to achieve.[17]

2

Jesus and Scripture according to Matthew's Gospel

Introduction

Matthew's Gospel is much longer than Mark's and contains all of Mark's quotations, along with about 30 more. Many of these are Matthew's own comment on the narrative (Matt. 1.23; 2.6, 15, 18, 23, etc.) rather than words of Jesus, and will only concern us in so far as they reveal Matthew's understanding of Jesus' use of Scripture. Most scholars believe that Matthew wrote his Gospel a few decades after Mark and indeed used Mark as one of his sources. This means that we can sometimes observe how Matthew has added, omitted or changed material from Mark, which will be important in Chapters 5–7, where we seek to reconstruct Jesus' use of Scripture. Of particular interest will be the source of Matthew's additions since this will have a significant effect on whether they should be considered reliable or not. But for this chapter we are simply enquiring about how Matthew understood Jesus' use of Scripture, and we begin with his portrayal of Jesus and the law.

Jesus and the law

Matthew includes all of the stories and quotations discussed in our chapter on Mark, but in addition he has two sections that are particularly significant for his understanding of Jesus and the law. The first is the temptation narrative (Matt. 4.1–11), where instead of the single statement that Jesus 'was in the wilderness for forty days, tempted by Satan' (Mark 1.13), Matthew has three specific temptations, each of which is answered by a quotation from Deuteronomy – see Table 2.1 overleaf.

As well as endorsing the authority of the law, the replies emphasize the point that the law is essentially about loyalty to God. In a different

Table 2.1

The temptation	Jesus' reply
The tempter came and said to him, 'If you are the Son of God, command these stones to become loaves of bread.'	'It is written, "One does not live by bread alone, but by every word that comes from the mouth of God."' (Deut. 8.3)
Then the devil took him to the holy city and placed him on the pinnacle of the temple, saying to him, 'If you are the Son of God, throw yourself down; for it is written, "He will command his angels concerning you", and "On their hands they will bear you up, so that you will not dash your foot against a stone."'	'Again it is written, "Do not put the Lord your God to the test."' (Deut. 6.16)
Again, the devil took him to a very high mountain and showed him all the kingdoms of the world and their splendour; and he said to him, 'All these I will give you, if you will fall down and worship me.'	'Away with you, Satan! for it is written, "Worship the Lord your God, and serve *only* him."' (Deut. 6.13)

context, Jesus will turn five loaves and two fishes into enough food to meet the needs of a large crowd (Matt. 14.13–21), but he will not perform such a miracle solely to meet his own needs. As with the second temptation, that would be tantamount to putting God to the test. The third temptation emphasizes the monotheistic foundation of Jewish belief, particularly as Matthew (or his source) has inserted the word 'only' into the quotation (see italics). It would appear that the context has affected the form of the quotation, since Jesus answers the devil's challenge by saying that one should 'worship the Lord your God', whereas Deuteronomy 6.13 speaks of 'fearing the LORD your God'. As in Mark, the authority of the law is not necessarily dependent on citing its precise wording. A further point to note is that the story not only demonstrates the authority of the law (it represents God's will), it is also a formidable defence against the temptations of the devil, something Matthew no doubt intends his readers to apply to their own lives.

The second major addition is the material included in the Sermon on the Mount (Matt. 5—7), the first of five discourses in Matthew's Gospel, all of which end with a formula such as 'when Jesus had finished saying these things' (Matt. 7.28; 11.1; 13.53; 19.1; 26.1). The arrangement is clearly deliberate and may reflect other notable collections of five books, such as the Pentateuch and Psalms. After the beatitudes ('Blessed are . . .') of Matt. 5.3–11, as well as a few other sayings (Matt. 5.14–16), Jesus insists that he has not come to abolish the law and the prophets but to fulfil them. Put another way, 'until heaven and earth pass away, not one letter, not one stroke of a letter, will pass from the law until all is accomplished' (Matt. 5.18). What this means for his disciples is that 'whoever breaks one of the least of these commandments, and teaches others to do the same, will be called least in the kingdom of heaven' (5.19). In the light of this it is probably significant that in Matthew's account of the hand-washing incident (15.1–20) there is no mention of 'cleansing all foods', and the final verse ('These are what defile a person, but to eat with unclean hands does not defile') clarifies that the discussion has not moved away from hand-washing rituals. This either represents a major difference between Matthew and Mark, or scholars such as James Crossley are correct to assert that Mark did not intend to abrogate the food laws and Matthew is simply removing an ambiguity, rather than correcting Mark's view.[1]

It is more difficult to decide what Matthew means by the word 'fulfil'. That he believed that Jesus fulfilled prophecy will become clear in the following section, 'Jesus and the prophets', but in what sense did Jesus fulfil the law? To answer this we must look at the next section of the Sermon on the Mount, traditionally known as the 'antitheses'. Here we have a series of statements from the law, introduced by such words as 'You have heard that it was said to those of ancient times' (Matt. 5.21, 33) or, more simply, 'You have heard that it was said' (Matt. 5.27, 38, 43) or 'It was also said' (Matt. 5.31). There then follows a comment by Jesus introduced by the words 'But I say to you' (Matt. 5.22, 28, 32, 34, 39, 44). The topics are murder, adultery, divorce (from the Ten Commandments) and oaths, retaliation and love of neighbour.

The first two can be seen as a fairly straightforward deepening of the commandments to include the corresponding attitudes of anger (which leads to murder) and lust (which leads to adultery). An illustration is offered for anger: 'So when you are offering your gift at the altar, if you remember that your brother or sister has something against you, leave your gift there before the altar and go; first be reconciled to your brother or sister, and then come and offer your gift' (Matt. 5.23–24). This is interesting in that while it gives priority to human relationships, it nevertheless implies that Christians will continue to offer gifts at the altar. Contrary to Paul's Gentile churches, it would appear that Matthew's church continues to uphold the ritual aspects of the law.

The antithesis on adultery is the shortest, and complements the later dispute with the Pharisees over the grounds for divorce (Matt. 19.3–12). What is of interest is that Matthew includes an exception clause ('anyone who divorces his wife, *except on the ground of unchastity*, causes her to commit adultery'), which is also found in his version of the dispute with the Pharisees ('And I say to you, whoever divorces his wife, *except for unchastity*, and marries another commits adultery'). This could be seen as a weakening of Jesus' original command, but in the light of the rigorous statements of Matthew 5.17–20 it is perhaps more likely that Matthew understood 'unchastity' (*porneia*) as already breaking the marriage bond; after all, it was punishable by death (John 7.53—8.11), although this was rarely enforced.

The antithesis about oaths ('You shall not swear falsely, but carry out the vows you have made to the Lord') draws on Leviticus 19.12 ('you shall not swear falsely by my name'), Numbers 30.2 ('When a man makes a vow to the LORD, or swears an oath to bind himself by a pledge, he shall not break his word') and Deuteronomy 23.21 ('If you make a vow to the LORD your God, do not postpone fulfilling it'). The antithesis, however, forbids the swearing of all such oaths and regards them as evil (Matt. 5.37).[2] As with the case of divorce, this represents the rigorous view in what was a live debate in contemporary Judaism. The enormity of failing to keep a vow made before God led in one of two directions: a growing reticence to swear oaths, as in Sirach 23.11 ('One who swears many oaths is full of iniquity, and the scourge will not leave his house'), or the use of circumlocutions ('I swear by heaven/the temple/Jerusalem') to avoid mentioning the name of God. Jesus forbids the latter and turns the former into an absolute: 'Do not swear at all, either by heaven, for it is the throne of God, or by the earth, for it is his footstool, or by Jerusalem, for it is the city of the great King.'

The criterion of dissimilarity

Along with the criterion of embarrassment, scholars have placed a good deal of weight on the so-called criterion of dissimilarity. Thus in the example on page 36 the absolute forbidding of oaths is unlike anything in contemporary Judaism and was not the practice of the early Church (Rom. 9.1; 2 Cor. 11.10–11; Gal. 1.20).[3] It therefore has a strong case for authenticity. The same is true of divorce, where both Matthew ('except on the grounds of unchastity') and Paul ('But if the unbelieving partner separates, let it be so' – 1 Cor. 7.15) clearly struggle to apply the absolute prohibition to their congregations. A less obvious example is the double command to love God and neighbour. Although both of these commands occur in Scripture, Judaism and the early Church, the precise formulation of them as 'first commandment' and 'second commandment', and the statement that there is 'no other commandment greater than these', is unique.[4] It should be noted that the material this criterion helps to authenticate is not necessarily more *characteristic* of the historical Jesus than material that sounds like 'normative Judaism'. It is simply that material that does pass this rigorous criterion has a good chance of being authentic.

Jesus' command to 'turn the other cheek' (Matt. 5.39) is perhaps the best known of all his teaching. It follows a quotation ('An eye for an eye and a tooth for a tooth') from either Exodus 21.24, Leviticus 24.20 or Deuteronomy 19.21 that sought to limit retaliation to that which had been suffered. As with the case of oaths and divorce, Jesus forbids what the law permits. However, this is not necessarily advocating a purely passive response to aggression. The striking on the right cheek is probably intended as an insult – as done by the glove in a different cultural setting – rather than as an act of violence. By offering the left cheek, one is refusing to accept the terms of the insult and is thus engaging in a form of passive resistance. Similarly, the person who forces you to go one mile with them – such as a soldier ordering you to carry his bags – wishes to end the transaction as the superior. By offering to go another mile, the balance changes, for the person is now in your debt, even if it goes unacknowledged.

The final antithesis is somewhat different in that the second part of the quotation ('You shall love your neighbour *and hate your enemy*') does not appear anywhere in the Old Testament. It may be a popular aphorism derived from texts like Deuteronomy 7.2 or 20.16. Thus the Qumran document known as the *Community Rule* opens with the exhortation to 'seek God with a whole heart and soul . . . [to] love all that he has chosen and hate all that he has rejected'. Jesus' response amounts to a definition of the word 'love' in Leviticus 19.18, which must extend beyond one's immediate family or work colleagues (tax collectors in the example). This appears to be a comment on the previous verse ('You shall not hate in your heart anyone *of your own kin*'), as perhaps the antithesis on retaliation was a comment of Leviticus 19.18a ('You shall not take vengeance or bear a grudge against *any of your people*').

The final verse (Matt. 5.48) brings to an end the six antitheses with the command 'Be perfect, therefore, as your heavenly Father is perfect.' This appears to echo Leviticus 19.2 ('You shall be holy, for I the LORD your God am holy'), but Matthew's use of 'perfect' (*teleios*) draws on the LXX of Deuteronomy 18.13, which reads 'You shall be perfect (*teleios*) before the Lord your God.' It is of interest that the advice given to the young man enquiring about eternal life is 'If you wish to be perfect (*teleios*), go, sell your possessions, and give the money to the poor' (Matt. 19.21). This could indicate that Jesus used an Aramaic word meaning 'perfect', but as we shall see in the next chapter, Luke's form of the saying is 'Be merciful, just as your Father is merciful' (6.36). Some scholars suggest that Jesus might have said both sayings, but others think that Matthew has chosen to translate the original Aramaic saying with *teleios* because that is what he wishes to emphasize.

There are two further texts that help clarify Matthew's understanding of Jesus and the law. In the debate concerning the greatest commandment (Matt. 22.34–40 = Mark 12.28–34), Matthew has a phrase that is not in Mark: 'On these two commandments hang all the law and the prophets' (Matt. 22.40). The word 'hang' (*krematai*) is used to describe crucifixion (Luke 23.39; Acts 5.30; 10.39; Gal. 3.13) and the millstone 'hung' around the neck of the one who causes the little ones to stumble (Matt. 18.6), but here it is clearly figurative. The law and the prophets 'hang' or are 'suspended' from the commandments to love God and neighbour, meaning either that they are deducible from them or inspired by them – or, as Robert Gundry suggests, both.[5]

In Matthew 23.23–24 Jesus castigates the scribes and Pharisees for tithing herbs while neglecting the 'weightier matters of the law: justice, mercy and faith'. But his conclusion is not that tithing herbs is of no importance but that they should have done these things *without* neglecting the more important matters. Thus the commands to love God and neighbour, as exemplified in justice, mercy and faith, do not *replace* the minutiae of the law but inspire and support them. Matthew values moral laws over cultic laws, but believes that the former inspire or direct the latter; they do not *abrogate* them.

Jesus and the prophets

We will begin with Matthew's two quotations from Hosea 6.6 since they are also relevant to his view of Jesus and the law. In his account of the call of Matthew the tax-collector – Mark 2.14 calls him Levi, though it is clearly the same event – there is an additional saying where Jesus says 'Go and learn what this means, "I desire mercy, not sacrifice"' (Matt. 9.13). Similarly, in his account of the disciples picking grain on the Sabbath, Matthew differs from Mark by including the following sayings:

> Or have you not read in the law that on the sabbath the priests in the temple break the sabbath and yet are guiltless? I tell you, something greater than the temple is here. But if you had known what this means, 'I desire mercy and not sacrifice', you would not have condemned the guiltless. (Matt. 12.5–7)

What is puzzling about these sayings is that neither incident is obviously about mercy or indeed about sacrifice. If the Hosea quotation had come in the story of the man with the withered hand, it would be more understandable: Mercy takes precedence over sacrifice or ritual obligation and so Jesus heals the man. But how is allowing the disciples to pick grain on the Sabbath an act of mercy? Perhaps the answer lies in another difference from the Markan account: Matthew says at the beginning of the story that the disciples were hungry (Matt. 12.1), so giving them permission to eat could be seen as an act of mercy, though there is no indication that they were actually starving. What is clear is that Matthew thinks the saying is of crucial importance since in both cases he stresses the need to *learn* what it means. As in Hosea, it does not mean that sacrifices are to be abandoned, which would contradict the saying in Matthew 5.24 ('be reconciled to your brother or sister, and then come and offer your gift'); rather it is stating that mercy – responding to need – is more important than ritual obligation, and is therefore similar to the comment of the scribe in Mark 12.33, that loving God and neighbour is 'much more important than all whole burnt offerings and sacrifices'.

Jesus and Isaiah

Matthew's use of Isaiah has a number of interesting features when compared with Mark. For example, instead of the composite quotation of Malachi 3.1/Exodus 23.20 and Isaiah 40.3 that opens Mark's Gospel ('See, I am sending my messenger . . . make his paths straight'), Matthew simply has the Isaiah quotation. But the Malachi/Exodus material has not been lost, for it occurs in a later passage, and this time it is a saying of Jesus. The whole episode is of great importance for understanding Jesus' use of Scripture – it also occurs in Luke, and many scholars believe it was therefore present in Q. However, we will focus at this point on how Matthew understands it.

Matthew 11 begins with John the Baptist sending a message to Jesus from prison: 'Are you the one who is to come, or are we to wait for another?' (v. 3). The question is understandable given John's apocalyptic message, since nothing much seems to have changed. Jesus replies by summarizing the miraculous deeds that are taking place, but in language that deliberately seems to echo texts from Isaiah – see Table 2.2.

Table 2.2

Matthew 11.4	Texts from Isaiah
Go and tell John what you hear and see: the blind receive their sight, the lame walk, the lepers are cleansed, the deaf hear,	On that day the deaf shall hear the words of a scroll, and out of their gloom and darkness the eyes of the blind shall see (29.18). Then the eyes of the blind shall be opened, and the ears of the deaf unstopped; then the lame shall leap like a deer, and the tongue of the speechless sing for joy (35.5–6).
the dead are raised,	Your dead shall live, their corpses shall rise (26.19).
and the poor have good news brought to them.	The spirit of the Lord GOD is upon me . . . to bring good news to the oppressed [NIV 'poor'] (61.1).

This is followed by Jesus calling John the Baptist a prophet (v. 9) and identifying him (v. 10) with the voice of Malachi 3.1/Exodus 23.20: 'See, I am sending my messenger ahead of you, who will prepare your way before you.' If that is the case, then Jesus is the one to whom such prophecies refer, as Matthew makes clear in the introduction ('When John heard in prison what *the Messiah* was doing'). Jesus can call John the greatest of the prophets, but even the least person in the kingdom of heaven is said to be greater than him (v. 11). In other words, Jesus is inaugurating a new age – or perhaps God is inaugurating a new age through Jesus – that surpasses everything that has gone before.

In the explanation of why Jesus speaks in parables, Matthew includes an abbreviated quotation of Isaiah 6.9 (as in Mark) but then reproduces the whole of Isaiah 6.9–10 as a separate quotation and in its Septuagintal form, which differs considerably from the Hebrew – see Table 2.3 overleaf.

Both Mark and Matthew have Jesus quote from Isaiah 6.9, with the two clauses in reverse order (looking before listening), but the correct order is given when Matthew has Jesus quote the text in full. It is also of interest that Matthew agrees with the LXX in the final line ('and I would heal them') whereas Mark has 'forgive' and uses a passive construction ('be forgiven'). Mark is in fact closer to the Aramaic translation and is thus likely to be closer to what Jesus actually said. Most scholars regard Matthew's fuller version as his own expansion to strengthen the connection with Isaiah 6.9–10. But it is interesting that when it comes to the incident where Jesus applies this to the disciples (Mark 8.17–18), Matthew only has 'Do you still not perceive? Do you not remember the five loaves . . .' (Matt. 16.9). It would appear that Matthew does not think that Jesus applied Isaiah 6.9–10 to the disciples, and this coheres with the additional words found after the explicit quotation: 'But blessed are your eyes, for they see, and your ears, for they hear' (Matt. 13.16). The almost perverse lack of comprehension of the disciples in Mark's Gospel is not shared by the other Gospels.

As we noted in the previous chapter, the connection between Jesus and Isaiah's servant is somewhat ambiguous in Mark. Matthew, however, has two specific quotations in which the identification is unequivocal. The first occurs just after Jesus has healed Peter's mother-in-law (Matt. 8.14–15/Mark 1.29–31). In the evening, the

Table 2.3

Isaiah 6.9–10 NETS	Matthew 13.13–15	Mark 4.11–12
Go, and say to this people:	The reason I speak to them in parables is that	but for those outside, everything comes in parables; in order that
'You will listen by listening, but you will not understand, and looking you will look, but you will not perceive.	'seeing they do not perceive, and hearing they do not listen, nor do they understand.'	'they may indeed look, but not perceive, and may indeed listen, but not understand;
	With them indeed is fulfilled the prophecy of Isaiah that says:	
	'You will indeed listen, but never understand, and you will indeed look, but never perceive.	
For this people's heart has grown fat, and with their ears they have heard heavily, and they have shut their eyes so that they might not see with their eyes and hear with their ears and understand with their heart and turn – and I would heal them.'	For this people's heart has grown dull, and their ears are hard of hearing, and they have shut their eyes; so that they might not look with their eyes, and listen with their ears, and understand with their heart and turn – and I would heal them.'	so that they may not turn again and be forgiven.'

people bring the sick and demon-possessed to Jesus and he heals them (Matt. 8.16/Mark 1.32–34). Matthew then has the statement that: 'This was to fulfil what had been spoken through the prophet Isaiah, "He took our infirmities and bore our diseases"' (Matt. 8.17). The words are from Isaiah 53.4, but Matthew has not followed the LXX, which speaks of 'bearing our sins', rather the Hebrew in referring to sickness in both phrases (infirmity/disease). Thus in contrast to later tradition (1 Pet. 2.24), Matthew applies Isaiah 53 to Jesus' healing ministry, not the salvific consequences of his death.

On another occasion, after the general statement that many 'crowds followed him, and he cured all of them' (Matt. 12.15), Matthew says that: 'This was to fulfil what had been spoken through the prophet Isaiah' (12.17), followed by a long quotation of Isaiah 42.1–4, which differs considerably from both the Hebrew text and the LXX:

> Here is my servant, whom I have chosen, my beloved, with whom my soul is well pleased. I will put my Spirit upon him, and he will proclaim justice to the Gentiles. He will not wrangle or cry aloud, nor will anyone hear his voice in the streets. He will not break a bruised reed or quench a smouldering wick until he brings justice to victory. And in his name the Gentiles will hope.   (Matt. 12.18–21)

The relevance of the quotation is not immediately apparent: Jesus is neither healing Gentiles nor procuring justice for them. What is clear is that Matthew wishes to make the identification of Jesus with Isaiah's servant explicit. A more relevant text might have been the LXX of Isaiah 61.1–3, where the anointed prophet preaches good news to the poor, heals the broken-hearted and opens the eyes of the blind. Matthew has already portrayed Jesus as alluding to this text in his reply to John the Baptist, and it may also lie behind the first three beatitudes ('Blessed are the poor in spirit . . . those who mourn . . . the meek'), especially as Isaiah 61.7 LXX speaks of 'inheriting the earth' (the promise given to the meek). As we shall see in the next chapter, Luke envisages Jesus as actually reading from Isaiah 61.1–2 in a synagogue service and declaring 'Today this scripture has been fulfilled in your hearing' (Luke 4.21). But it is not so clear that Matthew intends such an identification.

The text of the LXX known to Matthew

On a number of occasions Matthew quotes a form of the text that differs from both the Hebrew text that has come down to us (Masoretic Text) and the LXX represented in the majority of manuscripts. This could be because he is modifying the text to make his point or that he is quoting from memory and makes mistakes. However, at least in some instances it appears that he is quoting from a version of the LXX that differs from the principal manuscripts. From the evidence of the Dead

Sea Scrolls it would appear that there had been several attempts to revise the LXX text to bring it closer to the Hebrew text. In addition, we learn from the Scrolls that there were also variations in the Hebrew text, so that the question of what text Matthew was quoting from is extremely complicated. Given that we live in a period where there are countless English versions of the Bible, perhaps this should not be unduly surprising.[6]

Jesus and Zechariah

We saw in our last chapter that Mark records Jesus quoting Zechariah 13.7 ('I will strike the shepherd, and the sheep will be scattered') but does not draw attention to the identification of Jesus and the shepherd. Matthew, on the other hand, clearly thinks that the events leading up to Jesus' death are a fulfilment of the latter chapters of Zechariah. Thus as well as the quotation from Zechariah 13.7, he includes an explicit quotation of Zechariah 9.9 at Jesus' entry into Jerusalem: 'This took place to fulfil what had been spoken through the prophet, saying, "Tell the daughter of Zion, Look, your king is coming to you, humble, and mounted on a donkey, and on a colt, the foal of a donkey"' (Matt. 21.4–5). He also includes an explicit quotation of Zechariah 11.12–13 to explain Judas' betrayal of Jesus for 30 pieces of silver, though there are considerable difficulties with this text.[7]

These three explicit quotations demonstrate the importance of Zechariah to Matthew, and so it is of interest that before the quotation of Daniel 7.13 in the apocalyptic discourse (Mark 13.27; Matt. 24.30), he includes the following saying of Jesus: 'Then the sign of the Son of Man will appear in heaven, and then *all the tribes of the earth will mourn*' (Matt. 24.30). The latter phrase is a combination of Zechariah 12.10 ('they shall mourn him') and 12.14 (lit. 'all the tribes that are left'), with 'are left' replaced by 'of the earth'. Since this combination of Daniel 7.13 and Zechariah 12.10, 14 also occurs in Revelation 1.7 ('Look! He is coming with the clouds; every eye will see him, even those who pierced him; and on his account all the tribes of the earth will wail'), most scholars doubt that this goes back to Jesus. But what is clear is that

Matthew thought that Jesus understood his impending death and its consequences for Jerusalem in the light of Zechariah 9—14. As Clay Ham says:

> The messianic vision found in the prophetic oracles of Zechariah includes the restoration of the humble Davidic king, the smiting of the divinely appointed shepherd, the creation of a renewed remnant, and the worship of Yahweh by all nations. Matthew finds this prophetic presentation particularly compelling for his own representation of Jesus as the fulfillment of Zechariah's shepherd-king and the realization of Zechariah's eschatological hopes.[8]

Jesus and Jonah and Micah

There are two other references to the prophets that are worth mentioning. The first is a reference to the 'sign of Jonah', which occurs in Matthew 12.39 and 16.4. In both cases the context is the request for a sign from the 'scribes and Pharisees' (Matt. 12.38) or 'Pharisees and Sadducees' (Matt. 16.1), and in both cases Jesus replies with the words 'An evil and adulterous generation asks for a sign, but no sign will be given to it except the sign of (the prophet) Jonah.' In the latter passage the saying is left unexplained, but in the earlier passage, as well as adding 'Jonah the prophet', Jesus continues:

> For just as Jonah was three days and three nights in the belly of the sea monster, so for three days and three nights the Son of Man will be in the heart of the earth. The people of Nineveh will rise up at the judgement with this generation and condemn it, because they repented at the proclamation of Jonah, and see, something greater than Jonah is here! (Matt. 12.40–41)

This looks like it derives from the Church's proclamation of the death and resurrection of Jesus as the focal point of salvation and judgement. However, the tradition (1 Cor. 15.3–4) was that Jesus rose *on the third day* (counting Friday as the first day), which makes the time period ('three days *and* three nights') incorrect. Matthew uses 'on the third day' in each of the Passion predictions (Matt. 16.21; 17.23; 20.19), and so it is unlikely that he would invent a saying that contradicts this. The saying is followed by a reference to the queen of the south visiting Solomon, and ends with the phrase 'something greater than Solomon is here' (Matt. 12.42). Thus the purpose of the saying is to assert the superiority of Jesus over Jonah, whom tradition regarded as an extraordinary prophet, and Solomon, the acknowledged expert when it comes to wisdom. Indeed, Tom Wright goes as far as saying that to claim that he is greater than Solomon 'is to claim that he is the true Messiah; that he will build the eschatological Temple; that through him the Davidic kingdom will be restored'.[9]

Finally, there is a reference to Micah 7.6 concerning divisions in families. Jesus announces that he has not come to bring peace to the earth but a sword (Matt. 10.34). This comes as something of a surprise after the Sermon on the Mount, and is elaborated: 'For I have come to set a man against his father, and a daughter against her mother, and a daughter-in-law against her mother-in-law; and one's foes will be members of one's own household' (Matt. 10.35). The meaning can hardly be that Jesus *wishes* to set one member of the family against the other, but rather that this will be the effect of his mission. Families will be divided in their loyalties, as they were in Micah's day. It is interesting that this outcome would directly contradict Elijah's restoration programme in Malachi 4.6 ('He will turn the hearts of parents to their children and the hearts of children to their parents'), and that might be the reason why Matthew omits any reference to Scripture in his version of that story (Matt. 17.11–12).

Jesus and the writings

Matthew includes the references to Psalm 118.22–23 in the parable of the vineyard, Psalm 110.1 in the discussion about 'David's lord' and again in Jesus' reply to the high priest, and Psalm 22.1 as Jesus' cry from the cross. However, in each case, there is some additional material that has a bearing on how the psalm is to be understood. In the parable of the vineyard, the quotation about the rejected stone becoming the cornerstone is followed by the saying (according to most manuscripts[10]): 'Therefore I tell you, the kingdom of God will be taken away from you and given to a people that produces the fruits of the kingdom. The one who falls on this stone will be broken to pieces; and it will crush anyone on whom it falls' (Matt. 21.43–44). The first phrase clarifies the meaning of the words 'give the vineyard to others', by speaking of 'a people that produces the fruits of the kingdom'. The allegory has moved from tenants collecting fruit from

God's vineyard to people demonstrating the fruits of the kingdom in their own lives.

In the latter phrase, the rejected stone of the psalm is no longer being viewed as the cornerstone of a fine building but a stone that one can trip over or a stone that falls upon one. The stone that one can trip over is probably an allusion to the stumbling stone of Isaiah 8.14 since the two texts occur together in 1 Peter 2.6, along with Isaiah 28.16 ('See, I am laying in Zion a foundation stone, a tested stone, a precious cornerstone, a sure foundation: "One who trusts will not panic."'). It was evidently the practice of the early Church to bring these 'stone' texts together (Isaiah 8.14 and 28.16 are also combined in Romans 9.32–33), and that has probably influenced Matthew here. Indeed, the connection seems somewhat artificial as one is not usually 'broken to pieces' by tripping over a stone. On the other hand, one is 'crushed' if a heavy stone falls on one, and the latter phrase may be an allusion to the 'crushing stone' of Daniel 2.34–35. Many scholars believe that this reflects the 'search for texts' that characterized the early Church rather than actual sayings of Jesus.

In the debate about David's son, Mark uses an impersonal question ('How can the scribes say that the Messiah is the son of David?'), but Matthew has Jesus addressing them directly: 'What do you think of the Messiah? Whose son is he?' (Matt. 22.42). When they reply 'The son of David', Jesus then quotes the paradoxical Psalm 110.1. It is interesting that Matthew's quotation agrees with Mark that the enemies are to be put 'under your feet', whereas the LXX follows the Hebrew in saying that they are to be a 'footstool' for your feet. This could simply be a mistake, but it might have arisen because similar words occur in Psalm 8.6 ('You have given them dominion over the works of your hands; you have put all things *under* their feet'). However, as we shall see in the next chapter, Luke 'corrects' Mark and follows the wording of Psalm 110.1.

In the reply to the High Priest there is a slight difference that may nevertheless be significant. Before Jesus says 'you will see the Son of Man seated at the right hand of Power and coming on the clouds of heaven', he says 'from now on'. This seems to remove the possibility that he is talking about some distant event (whether the fall of Jerusalem or a second coming), and so is probably a reference to the resurrection. That will be the time when they will see that far from condemning Jesus, God has bestowed on him power and authority. Alternatively, the 'from now on you will see' could be taken to mean 'the next time you see me' and thus be indefinite – though this seems less likely.

In Matthew's account of the crucifixion, the taunt 'save yourself, and come down from the cross' now reads 'If you are the Son of God, come down from the cross' (Matt. 27.40). In addition, Matthew has the saying 'He trusts in God; let God deliver him now' (Matt. 27.43). Both sayings pick up the language of the temptation narrative (Matt. 4.1–11) and thus imply that the devil is using the bystanders to repeat his temptations. Matthew agrees with Mark that at three o'clock (the ninth hour) Jesus cries out with the words of Psalm 22.1, which he then translates as 'My God, my God, why have you forsaken me?' (Matt. 27.46). However, the quotation addresses God with the words 'Eli, Eli', while Mark has 'Eloi, Eloi'. Since 'Eli' is a transliteration of the Hebrew, one explanation for the difference is that Mark envisages Jesus crying out in Aramaic[11] whereas Matthew envisages the cry in Hebrew.

Of greater significance is that after Jesus has 'breathed his last' and the temple curtain is torn in two, Matthew says that the 'earth shook, and the rocks were split. The tombs also were opened, and many bodies of the saints who had fallen asleep were raised' (Matt. 27.51–52). Since this is not mentioned in any of the other Gospels or contemporary records, most scholars think that it represents Matthew's comment on the crucifixion. Far from remaining forsaken by God, the crucifixion is the event that triggers the resurrection of the dead. And what better way of illustrating this than picturing bodies rising from their tombs, in fulfilment of Ezekiel 37.12 ('Thus says the Lord GOD: I am going to open your graves, and bring you up from your graves, O my people; and I will bring you back to the land of Israel'). It is a matter of debate as to whether Matthew took this literally or was writing figuratively.

In addition to these psalm texts, Matthew has Jesus quoting from the psalms on three other occasions. In the Sermon on the Mount, Jesus says that there will be some who say 'Lord, Lord, did we not prophesy in your name?' who will hear the words 'I never knew you; go away from me, you evildoers' (Matt. 7.23). This does not sound like a quotation, but the Greek phrase for 'evildoers' is 'workers of lawlessness', which is only found in the Old Testament in Psalms

(Pss. 6.8; 14.4; 36.12; 53.4; 92.7, 9; 94.4; 119.3). In particular, Psalm 6.8 has David saying to the 'workers of lawlessness', 'depart from me', which is similar to Jesus' words here. Was this intentional on Matthew's part? Samuel Subramanian thinks so, commenting that the 'banishment pronounced in Ps. 6.9a LXX becomes an eschatological condemnation pronounced by Jesus against false prophets on the day of judgement'.[12] That Matthew thought that Jesus 'fulfilled' the psalms is shown by the quotation of Psalm 78.2 ('I will open my mouth to speak in parables') in Matthew 13.35. Matthew follows the parable of the sower with four other parables (seed growing secretly; weeds; mustard seed; yeast) and a further explanation of why Jesus speaks in parables. Significantly, the quotation from Psalm 78.2 is introduced with the words 'This was to fulfil what had been spoken through the *prophet*'. Matthew thinks of the psalms as prophecies, and it is Subramanian's view that this is also true for Mark and Luke.

Following the cleansing of the temple, Matthew says that children were crying out 'Hosanna to the Son of David' (Matt. 21.15). The chief priests and scribes were angry but Jesus defends them by quoting ('have you never read') Psalm 8.2 in the form: 'Out of the mouths of infants and nursing babies you have prepared praise for yourself' (Matt. 21.16). This agrees with the LXX, but the Hebrew speaks of 'strength' rather than 'praise'.[13] Once again the connection seems somewhat artificial since the story envisages children old enough to be present in the temple rather than 'babies'. But Robert Gundry suggests that it was probably enough for Matthew to see in the psalm a prophecy of 'youthful praise'.[14]

Finally, as well as the crowds shouting 'Blessed is the one who comes in the name of the Lord' during the triumphal entry (Matt. 21.9), Matthew has Jesus deliver a lament over Jerusalem ('Jerusalem, Jerusalem . . . How often have I desired to gather your children . . . your house is left to you, desolate') that ends with the words 'For I tell you, you will not see me again until you say, "Blessed is the one who comes in the name of the Lord"' (Matt. 23.39). To what does this refer? There is no hint in the apocalyptic discourse that follows (Matt. 24.4–31) that there is anything but judgement awaiting 'Jerusalem'. Can it refer to a distant 'second coming' of Jesus where 'Jerusalem' will welcome the Messiah? Subramanian says it does:

> Jesus was indeed acknowledged by some as the Messiah ... but he
> was ultimately rejected and crucified. At his second visitation, Jesus
> will come as the glorified representative of God; at that time, Israel
> will welcome him and fully accept his authority in fulfilment of
> Psalm 117(118).26a.[15]

However, there are difficulties with this view, not only because there
are significant doubts about whether Jesus ever referred to a 'second
coming', but because even if he did, there has been no suggestion
that this will have a positive outcome for Jerusalem. Perhaps Matthew
thought that the saying had been fulfilled in his own Jewish Christian
congregation, who have indeed welcomed Jesus as the Messiah and
continue to do so at every church service.

Conclusion

Although Mark stresses that Jesus was a great teacher (Mark 1.22),
he does not actually include much teaching in his Gospel (mainly in
chapters 4 and 13). Matthew demonstrates that Jesus was a great
teacher by having him deliver over 300 verses of teaching, arranged
in five sermons or discourses (Matt. 5—7, 10, 13, 18, 23—25). He
also has him debate matters of the law with the scribes and Pharisees
(e.g. oaths) and resist the devil's temptations by quoting three times
from the book of Deuteronomy. According to Matthew, Jesus insists
that he has not come to abolish the law but to fulfil it, and denounces
anyone who breaks even the least of the commandments. It is
true that in cases of conflict, moral laws take priority over ritual
laws (Matt. 12.5–7), but he undoubtedly envisages his followers
as law-abiding, as he himself was (Matt. 23.2–3). If it is true that
Matthew used Mark as one of his sources, we might regard this
additional material as secondary. But there are three reasons why
it has come to play an important role in determining Jesus' use of
Scripture:

1 Since some of this material is also found in Luke, it may come
  from Q and therefore belongs to the earliest strata of recoverable
  tradition.
2 The portrait of Jesus as a law-abiding Jew is very plausible in
  the light of everything else we know about Judaism in the first
  century.

3 It would explain why the early Church continued to follow the law and why there were such bitter disputes concerning the admission of Gentiles (Acts 10.14; 15.1).

In contrast, Matthew's much more explicit portrayal of Jesus' use of the prophets and psalms (which are treated as prophecies) looks like an attempt to make Jesus more 'Christian' by demonstrating that he was fully aware that Isaiah, Daniel and Zechariah spoke about him. That Matthew is willing to make such references more explicit can be seen in his use of Isaiah 6.9–10, where the brief allusion is followed by an explicit quotation, and one that follows the LXX. On the other hand, it should be noted that Jesus' reply to John the Baptist and his reference to being greater than Solomon and Jonah are both in Luke and may thus be part of Q. This does not prove their authenticity (there is still a gap of 20–30 years), but the burden of proof lies more with those who deny their authenticity than with those who accept it. In conclusion, Matthew offers a much fuller portrait of Jesus' use of Scripture than Mark, and even if some of this material is regarded as secondary, it suggests that our reconstruction must also draw on the later Gospels. There is much in Matthew and Luke that might be earlier than Mark, even though our knowledge of it only comes from these later Gospels.

3

Jesus and Scripture according to Luke's Gospel

Introduction

Unlike Matthew, Luke only has about two-thirds of Mark's quotations, partly because he does not include the stories about hand washing (Isa. 29.13), Corban (Exod. 20.12; 21.17), divorce (Gen. 1.27; 2.24) and the scattering of the disciples (Zech. 13.7), and partly because he has something different (comment on the vineyard parable, final words from the cross). On the other hand, he does include a number of the quotations found in Matthew but not in Mark, such as Jesus' response to the three temptations (Deut. 6.13, 16; 8.3), his reply to John the Baptist's question from prison (Isa. 26.19; 29.18; 35.5–6; 61.1), his application of Malachi 3.1/Exodus 23.20 to John (as opposed to Mark's Gospel, where it is a comment of the author), the sign of Jonah and division within families based on Micah 7.6. The most common explanation of this is that Luke had access to both Mark and Q, although the theory is not without its problems.[1] If it is correct that Q (or the earliest strata of Q) pre-dates Mark by around a decade, then this is our earliest source for the teaching of Jesus and is hence of great importance.

Jesus and the law

Luke shares with Matthew and Mark the story of the man with leprosy ('as Moses commanded, make an offering for your cleansing'), the twin stories of plucking grain on the Sabbath ('Have you not read what David did when he and his companions were hungry?') and the healing of the man with the withered hand ('I ask you, is it lawful to do good or to do harm on the Sabbath, to save life or to destroy it?'). The theme obviously appealed to Luke for he includes two other healing stories that make the same point. In Luke 13.10–17,

Jesus heals a woman who has been bent double for 18 years. The leader of the synagogue is indignant and says to the crowd: 'There are six days on which work ought to be done; come on those days and be cured, and not on the sabbath day' (13.14). But Jesus responds 'You hypocrites! Does not each of you on the sabbath untie his ox or his donkey from the manger, and lead it away to give it water? And ought not this woman, a daughter of Abraham whom Satan bound for eighteen long years, be set free from this bondage on the sabbath day?' (13.15–16). The analogy works better than rescuing an animal from a pit since healing the woman is not about responding to an emergency but showing mercy and kindness on the Sabbath.

In the following chapter (Luke 14.1–6), Jesus is eating a meal on the Sabbath with 'a leader of the Pharisees' when a man with dropsy (a water-retaining disease) appears. As with the man with the withered hand, Jesus challenges them: 'Is it lawful to cure people on the sabbath, or not?' (14.3). They do not answer and so Jesus cures the man and then asks, 'If one of you has a child or an ox that has fallen into a well, will you not immediately pull it out on a sabbath day?' (14.5). The analogy is not precise for the man has not just caught 'dropsy' and is not in immediate danger of dying; the healing could take place on the next day. However, what is interesting about Jesus' reply is that we know from the Dead Sea Scrolls (CD 11.13–17) that the Qumran community did indeed forbid such a rescue. John Meier concludes: 'Far from rejecting the sabbath, Jesus wished instead to make the sabbath livable for severely pressed Jewish peasants, who could hardly afford to stand by when they were in danger of losing one of their livestock, to say nothing of their children.'[2] With this in mind it is interesting to observe that whereas Matthew ends the sayings about not restricting love to those who can repay with the quotation 'Be perfect, therefore, as your heavenly Father is perfect' (Matt. 5.48), Luke has 'Be merciful, just as your Father is merciful' (Luke 6.36). Jesus is portrayed as keeping the Sabbath, but 'mercy' determines what can or cannot be done on it.

Luke includes the stories of the rich young man asking about eternal life (Luke 18.18–24), where Jesus recites the commandments (Luke puts adultery before murder), and the dispute with the Sadducees about resurrection, where the text 'I am the God of Abraham, the God of Isaac, and the God of Jacob' is used to show that the patriarchs are alive with God; Luke makes this more explicit by adding 'for to him all of them are alive' (Luke 20.38). However, he does not include the story where the scribe asks about the greatest commandment, probably because he has included an earlier story where another lawyer asks about eternal life and the man (rather than Jesus) cites the commandments to love God and neighbour. What is significant about this story is that the man goes on to ask, 'And who is my neighbour?', to which Jesus replies with the parable of the Good Samaritan:

> 'A man was going down from Jerusalem to Jericho, and fell into the hands of robbers, who stripped him, beat him, and went away, leaving him half dead. Now by chance a priest was going down that road; and when he saw him, he passed by on the other side. So likewise a Levite, when he came to the place and saw him, passed by on the other side. But a Samaritan while travelling came near him; and when he saw him, he was moved with pity. He went to him and bandaged his wounds, having poured oil and wine on them. Then he put him on his own animal, brought him to an inn, and took care of him. The next day he took out two denarii, gave them to the innkeeper, and said, "Take care of him; and when I come back, I will repay you whatever more you spend." Which of these three, do you think, was a neighbour to the man who fell into the hands of the robbers?' He said, 'The one who showed him mercy.' Jesus said to him, 'Go and do likewise.' (Luke 10.30–37)

The parable has often been understood as the need for love to cross boundaries and prejudices, but recent commentators have focused on the notion of corpse impurity. As the victim is described as 'half dead', the priest and Levite are presented 'as figures who choose to maintain purity rather than carry out the obligations of the love command in a situation where obedience only to one is possible'.[3] On this interpretation, the demands of mercy override the demands of purity. Bill Loader offers this summary of the three versions of the story found in the Gospels:

> His Markan source had the lawyer ask at a more theoretical level about which commandment was greatest (Mark 12:28). Luke has no interest in such distinctions. His focus is not to affirm a hierarchy among the commandments, either in an inclusive sense, as Matthew, or an exclusive one, which sets aside some parts of the Law, like Mark. All God's commandments are to be obeyed! Luke's focus is on doing.[4]

On the other hand, the priest and Levite are said to be *going down* from Jerusalem, suggesting that their temple service was over. James Crossley therefore suggests that Jesus might be challenging *halaka* traditions that were seeking to extend the purity laws beyond that which is prescribed in Scripture.[5]

Luke has a number of stories in common with Matthew that are not in Mark. He has the three temptations, though the order of the second and third is reversed. Since Luke begins and ends this section with reference to Jesus being full of the Holy Spirit (Luke 4.1, 14), it is possible that he understands Jesus' responses to the temptations in terms of 'inspiration' rather than 'exegesis'. This is perhaps supported by the way that Luke has used the material concerning retaliation (Luke 6.29–30) and love of enemies (Luke 6.27–28, 32–36), which are not part of any 'antitheses' or quotations from Scripture but free-standing teaching. Thus it may be that Matthew is responsible for putting this material into an exegetical framework rather than Jesus.

On the other hand, Luke does include the saying about it being easier for heaven and earth to pass away than 'one stroke of a letter in the law to be dropped' (Luke 16.17). He does not have the material about the one who breaks the least of the commands being called least in the kingdom (Matt. 5.17–20), but he does include the saying that the Pharisees should not have neglected 'justice and the love of God' in their preoccupation with tithing herbs (Luke 11.42). As in Matthew, the point is not that 'justice and the love of God' replaces the tithing of herbs but that they should have done these things without neglecting the more important matters.

Just before the saying about the 'stroke of a letter' not passing away, Luke has a saying about the law and the prophets being 'in effect until John came' (Luke 16.16). This puzzling saying, which could suggest that the law and the prophets are no longer in effect, is also found in Matthew, but in a different form and in a different place. In Luke the possibility that the law and the prophets are no longer in force is immediately denied by the saying that not one stroke of the law is to be dropped. In between these two sayings is a straightforward clause (since John, the kingdom is being proclaimed) and a puzzling one ('everyone tries to enter it by force'). In Matthew, the saying about the 'stroke of the law' occurs in the Sermon on the Mount (Matt. 5.18), but later, in Matthew 11, he also has a saying that links the kingdom with violence, which is followed by a saying about the law and the prophets being in force until John. It is worth seeing the texts in parallel, along with their location – see Table 3.1.

There are two main theories to account for these similarities and differences. The first is that Luke rearranged the material from Matthew. On this view, Luke closely followed Matthew in recording the four sections about John the Baptist (Luke 7.18–28/Matt. 11.2–11) but replaced the two sayings about the kingdom suffering violence and the law and prophets being until John because, first, he wished to include a parenthetical summary condemning the Pharisees (Luke

Table 3.1

Luke 15—16	Matthew 11	Luke 7
Lost sheep and coin (15.1–10)	*John's question to Jesus (11.2–3)*	*John's question to Jesus (7.18–21)*
Prodigal son (15.11–32)	*Tell him about the signs (11.4–6)*	*Tell him about the signs (7.22–23)*
Unjust manager (16.1–13)	*John is the messenger (11.7–10)*	*John is the messenger (7.24–27)*
Hypocrisy of Pharisees (16.14–15)	*No one greater than John (11.11)*	*No one greater than John (7.28)*
'The law and the prophets were in effect until John came; since then the good news of the kingdom of God is proclaimed, and everyone tries to enter it by force. But it is easier for heaven and earth to pass away, than for one stroke of a letter in the law to be dropped' (16.16–17)	'From the days of John the Baptist until now the kingdom of heaven has suffered violence, and the violent take it by force. For all the prophets and the law prophesied until John came; and if you are willing to accept it, he is Elijah who is to come' (11.12–14)	(And all the people who heard this, including the tax collectors, acknowledged the justice of God, because they had been baptized with John's baptism. But by refusing to be baptized by him, the Pharisees and the lawyers rejected God's purpose for themselves.) (7.29–30)
Rich man and Lazarus (16.19–31)	*Playing the flute for you (11.16–17)* *Glutton and drunkard (11.18–19)*	*Playing the flute for you (7.31–32)* *Glutton and drunkard (7.33–35)*

7.29–30) and, second, he wished to include these sayings before the parable of the rich man and Lazarus, which concludes: 'If they do not listen to Moses and the prophets, neither will they be convinced even if someone rises from the dead' (Luke 16.31).

The second, more common theory is that both Matthew and Luke have used Q. Matthew has chosen to use the 'one stroke of the law' saying as an introduction to the 'antitheses' in his Sermon on the Mount (Matt. 5.18), and the 'until John' sayings in the major discussion about John the Baptist in chapter 11. Luke has chosen to use the 'until John' sayings in his section on parables, and adds the 'one stroke of the law' saying to avoid the implication that the law is no longer in force. If this is correct, then in order to ascertain Jesus' use of Scripture we have to decouple the sayings from their context in Matthew and Luke (recognizing that one of them could have preserved the original setting), and reconstruct the most plausible setting.

Critical editions of Q

If the wording and context of Matthew and Luke is identical, then it is likely to be the wording and context of Q (or a huge coincidence). But if the wording and context differ, then scholars have to decide which is closest to Q and hence (probably) closest to the historical Jesus. There are two main ways of doing this. First, if the difference coincides with language that is typical of one of the Gospels, then the probability lies with the other. Second, if the wording seems to serve the interests of one of the Gospels, then the probability lies with the other. For example, it is easily demonstrated that Matthew wishes to portray Jesus as an exegete of Scripture (like himself), and so his use of the 'one stroke of the law' saying as an introduction to the 'antitheses' is less likely than Luke's context. On this basis, scholars have reconstructed what they consider to be the original wording of Q and published the results in a series of critical editions.[6] By convention, a reference to a Q saying such as Q 7.22 refers to the text behind Luke 7.22 and its parallel in Matthew (in this case, Matt. 11.4).

Jesus and the prophets

The outstanding feature of Luke's portrayal of Jesus and the prophets is the incident in the synagogue recorded in Luke 4.16–30. Both

Matthew and Mark record a rejection of Jesus in his home town of Nazareth (Mark 6.1–6/Matt. 13.54–58), but Luke narrates a rejection at the beginning of the Gospel and gives it a specific setting: Jesus is asked to read in the synagogue and is given the scroll of the prophet Isaiah. It is unclear whether Luke wishes his readers to understand that Jesus unrolled the scroll until he found (what we know as) Isaiah 61 or whether it was the reading for the day.[7] Either way, what follows is not a reading from any known text of Isaiah 61 but a conflation of the lxx[8] of Isaiah 61.1–2 (omitting 'to heal the brokenhearted') with a phrase from Isaiah 58.6 ('let the oppressed go free') – see Table 3.2.

Since Luke goes on to record Jesus as declaring 'Today this scripture has been fulfilled in your hearing' (Luke 4.21), it is clear that Luke understands Jesus to be claiming that he is the anointed prophet of Isaiah 61. This also offers a different perspective on the proverb about a prophet not being welcome in his home town. Both Matthew and Mark end their rejection stories with a well-known proverb: 'Prophets are not without honour except in their own country' (Matt. 13.57/ Mark 6.4). But when this same proverb is cited in Luke, it comes

Table 3.2

Isaiah 61.1–2 NETS	*Isaiah 58.6* NETS	*Luke 4.18–19* NRSV
The Spirit of the Lord is upon me, because he has anointed me; he has sent me to bring good news to the poor, *to heal the brokenhearted*, to proclaim release to the captives and recovery of sight to the blind,	I have not chosen such a fast, says the Lord, rather loose every bond of injustice; undo the knots of contracts made by force; *let the oppressed go free*, and tear up every unjust note.	The Spirit of the Lord is upon me, because he has anointed me to bring good news to the poor. He has sent me to proclaim release to the captives and recovery of sight to the blind,
to summon the acceptable year of the Lord and the day of retribution, to comfort all who mourn.		*to let the oppressed go free*, to proclaim the year of the Lord's favour.

after the identification of Jesus with Isaiah 61, suggesting that it is not so much about the rejection of any prophet but the rejection of God's anointed prophet.

It is difficult to know what to make of the form of the Isaiah reading cited by Luke. It is hard to think of any reason why Luke would exclude the phrase 'to heal the brokenhearted', which fits so well with his understanding of Jesus. Perhaps the text that he was using was corrupt at this point. On the other hand, Charles Kimball thinks that the insertion of a phrase from Isaiah 58.6 was deliberate and reflects the sermon or homily that would normally follow the reading:

> In the linking of these texts, Jesus defined his ministry in terms of OT prophecy and fulfillment: he cited Isa. 61.1–2 to claim that he was the herald who proclaimed the messianic release and inserted Isa. 58.6d to emphasize that he was also the agent of this spiritual liberation.[9]

Michael Prior makes a different point. He believes that the reference to Isaiah 58.6 intensifies the social dimension of the prophetic message and provides a striking corrective to any religious practice that neglects the plight of the needy. Thus Luke places this story at the beginning of his Gospel to introduce the key theme of Jesus' ministry – liberation. By placing the story at the beginning, it functions as an interpretative lens through which the rest of the Gospel is to be understood.[10]

As well as identifying Jesus with the anointed prophet of Isaiah 61, Luke also makes the association with the suffering servant of Isaiah 53 explicit by having Jesus directly quote from it. After the words of institution at the last supper (Luke 22.17–20), Luke has Jesus ask the disciples, 'When I sent you out without a purse, bag, or sandals, did you lack anything?' (Luke 22.35). They replied 'No, not a thing.' Jesus then adds the enigmatic saying that 'the one who has no sword must sell his cloak and buy one', followed by a quotation from Isaiah 53.12 ('And he was counted among the lawless'). The quotation is intro-duced by 'For I tell you, this scripture must be fulfilled in me', to which is added 'and indeed what is written about me is being fulfilled'. What is interesting about this is that although Luke thinks Jesus directly applied Isaiah 53 to himself, he does not draw out any of the 'salvific' potential of that chapter (such as verse 10, 'When you make his life an offering for sin'). As it stands, Jesus cites the words to indicate that he is to die among criminals and that this was the path set out for him. There is no indication that Jesus is contemplating a death that is 'on their behalf'.[11]

If the associations with Isaiah 53 and 61 are more explicit in Luke than the other Gospels, the association with Isaiah 6.9–10 is more muted. Luke agrees with Mark that the *purpose* of the parables (rather than the result, as in Matthew) is blindness and deafness, but abbreviates the quotation. As a result the reader could easily miss the fact that the words are taken from Isaiah at all: 'I speak in parables, so that looking they may not perceive, and listening they may not understand' (Luke 8.10). One explanation for this is that Luke is generally thought to be the author of the book of Acts (cf. Luke 1.1–4 and Acts 1.1), and that book ends with Paul reflecting on his ministry and citing Isaiah 6.9–10 as an explanation for the failure of the majority of the Jews to believe. Thus by muting the saying in the Gospel, Luke indicates that the prophesied blindness and deafness *began* in Jesus' day and was completed by the end of Acts.

In the story of the cleansing of the temple, Luke agrees with Matthew rather than Mark that the quotation from Isaiah 56.7 was 'My house shall be called a house of prayer', omitting the phrase 'for all the nations'. This is surprising given Luke's interest in Gentiles, but Christopher Evans suggests that Luke may have omitted it because he does not believe that the salvation of the nations involves a pilgrimage to the temple; rather, the gospel will go out to them, as Acts 1.8 makes clear.[12]

In the parable of the vineyard, Luke only quotes Psalm 118.22 ('The stone that the builders rejected has become the cornerstone'), omitting the following verse that it was 'the LORD's doing, and it is amazing in our eyes'. But he does agree with Matthew that this was followed by two further 'stone' sayings: 'Everyone who falls on that stone will be broken to pieces; and it will crush anyone on whom it falls' (Luke 20.18) – see Table 3.3.

The result is that Luke's emphasis is much more on 'rejection' rather than 'transfer of ownership' (Mark) or 'transfer of ownership followed by judgement' (Matthew). Can we say which is more likely to be closer to what Jesus said? A *maximalist* answer is that Jesus said all of these sayings, but Mark and Luke have chosen to omit some of them. Thus Charles Kimball thinks that he can say rather precisely how Jesus used Scripture in this story:

Table 3.3

Matthew 21.42–44	Mark 12.10–11	Luke 20.17–18
Have you never read in the scriptures: 'The stone that the builders rejected has become the cornerstone; this was the Lord's doing, and it is amazing in our eyes'? Therefore I tell you, the kingdom of God will be taken away from you and given to a people that produces the fruits of the kingdom. The one who falls on this stone will be broken to pieces; and it will crush anyone on whom it falls.	Have you not read this scripture: 'The stone that the builders rejected has become the cornerstone; this was the Lord's doing, and it is amazing in our eyes'?	What then does this text mean: 'The stone that the builders rejected has become the cornerstone'? Everyone who falls on that stone will be broken to pieces; and it will crush anyone on whom it falls.

Jesus employed the OT in a typological and prophetic manner in this exposition. He made a *pesher*-like claim to be the OT's rejected and judging stone, and he pictured himself as a type of rejected servant of God who, due to his sonship, is in a different class than the previous servants.[13]

On the other hand, a *minimalist* answer is that Jesus said none of these sayings. The parable had one purpose, and that was to condemn the tenants for their shocking behaviour. It was part of Jesus' sweeping critique of exploitation – in this case, the common practice of absentee landlords. The addition of Psalm 118.22 turned this into something positive, by saying that the rejected stone has become the cornerstone of a new building. John Kloppenborg argues that the connection is quite artificial (stone not son) and becomes even more so when Matthew and Mark add Psalm 118.23 ('this was the Lord's doing, and it is amazing in our eyes'), implying that the whole sorry story was in fact part of God's plan to give the vineyard to others.

In between these two positions a *moderate* view is that Jesus purposely drew on the vineyard allegory of Isaiah 5 but introduced a new feature: the landlord repeatedly sent servants to 'collect' the fruit. The servants are a fairly obvious reference to the prophets who urged Israel to return to God and bear fruit (justice, righteousness, mercy). Jesus thus identified himself with God's mission to bring Israel to repentance and prepare for the coming kingdom of God (see Mark 1.15). After the resurrection, the parable was elaborated so that the landlord additionally sent his 'beloved son', who is killed and the vineyard transferred to others (the Church). Since this would require defence, the Scripture quotations were added to show that this transfer has always been God's plan, while the destiny of 'unbelieving Israel' is to be 'crushed'. How we decide between the maximalist, minimalist and moderate positions will be discussed in Chapters 5–7.

The criterion of multiple attestation

We can have more confidence in the historicity of an event if it is attested by more than one source. However, this is only true if the sources are independent. The authenticity of the quotation from Psalm 118.22 is not increased by stating that it occurs in three Gospels, since the majority of scholars believe that Matthew and Luke took it from Mark. However, the probability is increased by noting that it also occurs in the non-canonical *Gospel of Thomas*. This document has proved difficult to date, estimates ranging from 60 to 150 CE, but whatever the date, it does not appear to know Mark's Gospel. Thus the psalm quotation has multiple attestation (Mark, *Gospel of Thomas*), which adds to the case for authenticity. It should be noted, however, that just because an event is only known from one source, it does not necessarily mean that it is inauthentic. The point is simply that the probability increases if multiple attestation can be demonstrated.

Like Matthew, Luke includes the 'sign of Jonah' tradition, and most scholars believe it was in Q. However, Luke does not include the saying about the three days and three nights, which raises the question of whether it was in Q and he omitted it, or was not in Q and Matthew added it. Given that it differs from the tradition that Jesus was raised *on the third day*, it is unlikely that Matthew added it, and so he probably found it in Q. Luke's summary ('For just as Jonah became a sign to the people of Nineveh, so the Son of Man will be to this generation') can then be understood as his attempt to replace the saying and also form a bridge to the sayings about the queen of the South and Nineveh, which, as Table 3.4 shows, are almost identical (see italics) but appear in the opposite order.

At Jesus' trial before the chief priests (Luke 22.69), Luke differs from Matthew and Mark in the manner in which he presents the composite quotation of Daniel 7.13 and Psalm 110.1. Luke does

Table 3.4

Matthew 12.38–42	*Luke 11.29–32*
Then some of the scribes and Pharisees said to him, 'Teacher, we wish to see a sign from you.' But he answered them, 'An evil and adulterous generation asks for a sign, but no sign will be given to it except the sign of the prophet Jonah. For just as Jonah was for three days and three nights in the belly of the sea monster, so for three days and three nights the Son of Man will be in the heart of the earth.	When the crowds were increasing, he began to say, 'This generation is an evil generation; it asks for a sign, but no sign will be given to it except the sign of Jonah. For just as Jonah became a sign to the people of Nineveh, so the Son of Man will be to this generation.
'The people of Nineveh will rise up at the judgement with this generation and condemn it, because they repented at the proclamation of Jonah, and see, something greater than Jonah is here!	'The queen of the South will rise at the judgement with *the people* of this generation and condemn *them*, because she came from the ends of the earth to listen to the wisdom of Solomon, and see, something greater than Solomon is here!
'The queen of the South will rise up at the judgement with this generation and condemn it, because she came from the ends of the earth to listen to the wisdom of Solomon, and see, something greater than Solomon is here!'	'The people of Nineveh will rise up at the judgement with this generation and condemn it, because they repented at the proclamation of Jonah, and see, something greater than Jonah is here!'

not say that the priests will *see* the Son of Man seated at the right hand of Power but simply states it as a fact ('the Son of Man *will be* seated at the right hand of the power of God'). Neither does he have the phrase about 'coming on/with the clouds of heaven', which makes the link with Daniel 7.13 much less explicit. This is consistent with his use of these traditions in the apocalyptic discourse (Luke 21), where the phrase 'the Son of Man coming in a cloud' is less obviously connected with Daniel 7.13 than Matthew's 'coming on the clouds of heaven'.

Jesus and the writings

The most significant difference in Luke's portrayal of Jesus' use of the writings comes in the crucifixion story. Instead of the opening words of Psalm 22 ('My God, my God, why have you forsaken me?'), Luke has Jesus say 'Father, into your hands I commend my spirit', a quotation from Psalm 31.5. When this is coupled with the fact that only Luke includes the dialogue with the two criminals and the promise to the penitent ('Truly, I tell you, today you will be with me in Paradise' – Luke 23.43), it is clear that he envisages a much more positive end to Jesus' life than Matthew or Mark. One suggestion for why he might not have wanted to present Jesus as forsaken is that in his companion work – Acts – he has Peter offer a scriptural argument for Jesus' resurrection based on Psalm 16. The argument turns on the phrase 'For you will not *forsake* my soul to Hades or let your holy one see corruption', which cannot refer to David as he died and his body did see corruption; so it must apply to someone else, namely Jesus ('the holy one'). This would hardly be convincing if, shortly before this, Jesus cried out 'My God, my God, why have you *forsaken* me?'

Despite this major difference, there is an interesting coincidence in vocabulary between Mark and Luke. Both end the crucifixion story by saying that Jesus 'expired', using the Greek verb *ekpneo*. This verb is not found anywhere else in the New Testament or the LXX, and means literally 'out-breathed'. Thus it would seem that while Luke passes over Mark's forsaken saying, he takes the rare verb *ekpneo* as a clue to a different sort of quotation, one that has Jesus offering up his spirit to God. He might even have supposed that Jesus *must* have quoted this text in the act of expiring.[14]

Conclusion

Luke ends his Gospel with Jesus explaining to a group of disciples on the road to Emmaus and his own disciples in Jerusalem that the Scriptures had to be fulfilled in him:

> 'Oh, how foolish you are, and how slow of heart to believe all that the prophets have declared! Was it not necessary that the Messiah should suffer these things and then enter into his glory?' Then beginning with Moses and all the prophets, he interpreted to them the things about himself in all the scriptures. (Luke 24.25–27)

> 'These are my words that I spoke to you while I was still with you – that everything written about me in the law of Moses, the prophets, and the psalms must be fulfilled.' Then he opened their minds to understand the scriptures, and he said to them, 'Thus it is written, that the Messiah is to suffer and to rise from the dead on the third day, and that repentance and forgiveness of sins is to be proclaimed in his name to all nations, beginning from Jerusalem.' (Luke 24.44–47)

It is clear Luke believes that all the Scriptures point to Jesus, and that during his final days on earth he explained this to his disciples. More specifically, he believes that Jesus explained how the Scriptures speak of a Messiah who must first suffer and then enter into his glory. Had this come at the end of Matthew or Mark we would perhaps conclude that Jesus was referring to the Zechariah saying ('I will strike the shepherd'), the ransom saying ('give his life a ransom for many') or Psalm 22.1 ('why have you forsaken me?') as texts that predict his suffering. But none of these quotations appear in Luke. It could refer to the 'stone that the builders rejected' (Ps. 118.22) at the end of the parable of the vineyard, but Luke's emphasis is much more on the stone crushing others than the stone's suffering. This leaves the quotation of Isaiah 53.12 ('And he was counted among the lawless'), though this seems a weak basis for asserting that Scripture teaches that the Messiah must first suffer.

If Luke does not intend these summary statements to point back to any of the specific quotations used in his Gospel, perhaps he means that the 'narrative' of Scripture speaks of suffering followed by glory. Whether it is Israel's history, as exemplified by the exodus (slavery followed by promised land) or the exile (captivity followed by return to promised land), or the experience of an individual, such as David in the psalms or the servant in Isaiah, the pattern of suffering and deliverance is woven into Scripture. In a secular idiom, we might say that there is 'no gain without pain'. Scripture tells a story of suffering and redemption, which is to be the vocation of the one who represents Israel and acts on behalf of humanity. As Tom Wright says, Jesus evoked the 'second-Temple story of the suffering and exile of the people of YHWH in a new form, and proceeded to act it out . . . symbolically to undergo the fate he had announced, in symbol and word, for Jerusalem as a whole'.[15]

4

Jesus and Scripture according to
John's Gospel

Introduction

Matthew, Mark and Luke are referred to as the Synoptic Gospels because they can be 'seen together' (the meaning of the Greek *syn-opsis*). In other words, despite their differences, they follow the same basic storyline: baptism and temptation, appointment of the twelve, healings, exorcisms and parables in Galilee, Peter's confession, teaching on suffering ('Son of Man'), rich young ruler, triumphal entry, cleansing of the temple, vineyard parable, apocalyptic discourse, last supper, Gethsemane, arrest and crucifixion. And as we have seen, they share a common stock of scriptural quotations from the law (Exod. 3.6; 20.12–16; Lev. 19.18; Deut. 6.4), the prophets (Isa. 6.9–10; 56.7; Jer. 7.11; Dan. 7.13) and the writings (Pss. 110.1; 118.22).

John's Gospel is very different. Very few of the stories mentioned above appear in John, and none of these quotations appear on the lips of Jesus, though the author tells us that the unbelief of the Jews was in fulfilment of Isaiah 6.9–10 (John 12.39–40). Instead, the only explicit quotations spoken by Jesus concern his status as the 'bread of life' in John 6.25–59 (Isa. 54.13), the title 'Son of God' in 10.31–39 (using Psalm 82.6), Judas' betrayal in 13.18–20 as a fulfilment of Psalm 41.9, and the world's hatred of Jesus in 15.18–25 as a fulfilment of Psalm 69.4. For this reason, we will not divide our discussion into the three categories of law, prophets and writings but consider each of these quotations in turn, followed by a summary of the allusions and general references to Scripture in John.

Were the Gospels written by eyewitnesses?

None of the Gospels indicate who wrote them, but the early Church believed that they came from eyewitnesses who could therefore vouch for their authenticity. Matthew and John were thought to be written by the apostles Matthew and John, who would therefore have been eyewitnesses to most of the events recorded in their Gospels (the infancy stories being the obvious exception). Mark and Luke were not eyewitnesses, but Mark was thought to have drawn on Peter's preaching, while Luke was an associate of Paul's (though it is unclear how this helps since Paul was not present during Jesus' ministry). Some scholars appeal to this tradition to suggest that we should trust what the Gospels tell us unless there are good reasons for not doing so (the 'burden of proof' argument).[1] Others, however, believe that the differences between the Gospels, particularly between the Synoptic Gospels and John, are 'good reasons' for doubting the authenticity of the material unless there is evidence to support authenticity. If John's Gospel comes from an eyewitness who heard Jesus openly proclaiming his divinity and the promise of eternal life, it is startling that his fellow eyewitness (Matthew) chose to omit most of it.

The four explicit quotations

John 6.25–59

Matthew, Mark and Luke all have the story of the feeding of the 5,000 (Matt. 14.13–21; Mark 6.30–44; Luke 9.10–17), and Matthew and Mark follow it by a story of Jesus walking on water (Matt. 14.22–33; Mark 6.45–52). John also has the feeding of the 5,000 and the walking on water, but follows it by a long discourse about Jesus as the 'bread of life that came down from heaven' (John 6.51). There is nothing like this in the Synoptic Gospels, and by the time we get to John 6.54 ('Those who eat my *flesh* and drink my *blood* have eternal life') we are clearly reflecting the Eucharistic teaching of the early Church (the original miracle concerned bread and fishes, not bread and wine). For this reason, very few scholars would include anything from this section in their reconstruction of Jesus' use of Scripture, though it is significant for determining how John understood it.

The discourse begins with Jesus accusing the crowd for following him only because they enjoyed eating the bread. He urges them not to 'work for the food that perishes, but for the food that endures for eternal life' (John 6.27). This puts them in mind of the manna that sustained the Israelites in the desert, and they quote from either Exodus 16.4 ('I am going to rain bread from heaven for you') or the reflection of this event in Psalm 78.24 ('he rained down on them manna to eat, and gave them the grain of heaven'). Jesus then makes the point that it was not Moses who gave them this bread, but 'my Father who gives you the true bread from heaven' (John 6.32). They are interested, and ask Jesus to give them this bread, but when he explains to them that he himself is the bread of life, they take offence. He then quotes from Isaiah 54.13 ('And they shall all be taught by God') before introducing the crux of his interpretation: 'Your ancestors ate the manna in the wilderness, and they died. This is the bread that comes down from heaven, so that one may eat of it and not die' (John 6.49–50). Because the Israelites died, the manna could not have been the promised 'bread from heaven'; rather, this is fulfilled in Jesus.

Peder Borgen has argued that the form of this discourse resembles the homilies of Philo and other Jewish writings.[2] They typically begin with a quotation from the law, then expound its key words with the help of a prophetic text, and conclude by returning to the text from the law. In this case the key text (Exod. 16.4) is spoken by the crowd, but what follows is an explanation/clarification of who gave the bread (God, not Moses), the nature of the bread (it gives eternal life, not just ordinary life) and the origin of the bread (it is from the Father, not just from heaven – that is, the sky). The prophetic text (Isa. 54.13) introduces the idea of being taught by God, and after further clarifications, Jesus returns to the Exodus text ('This is the bread that comes down from heaven').

It is an interesting theory, but the similarities are only partial. Indeed, Maarten Menken has argued that the initial text is more likely to be Psalm 78.24, where the third person pronoun ('*he* rained down on them manna') is not specified and hence open to speculation and exegesis.[3] One might also have expected rather more to be made of the prophetic text, perhaps equating Jesus' teaching with the 'bread of life'. As it is, it does not play much of a role in the rest of the exposition. It would appear that John wishes to portray Jesus as expositing Scripture in the manner of a religious expert, but its characteristic feature is Christological, an exposition of his own role in the fulfilment of the text.

John 10.31–39

After a long discourse on sheep and shepherds, where Jesus identifies himself as the good shepherd who 'lays down his life for the sheep' (John 10.11), the Jews take up stones to kill him (John 10.31). We then read of the following exchange:

> 'I have shown you many good works from the Father. For which of these are you going to stone me?' The Jews answered, 'It is not for a good work that we are going to stone you, but for blasphemy, because you, though only a human being, are making yourself God.' Jesus answered, 'Is it not written in your law, "I said, you are gods"? If those to whom the word of God came were called "gods" – and the scripture cannot be annulled – can you say that the one whom the Father has sanctified and sent into the world is blaspheming because I said, "I am God's Son"?'
> (John 10.32–36)

There are several things that are puzzling about this. First, the quotation comes from Psalm 82.6 but is introduced as coming from the law. This is unlikely to be a mistake, and the probable explanation is that 'law' is being used generically to mean 'Scripture'. However, what is startling is that Jesus refers to it as '*your* law', as if it were no longer *his* law. Some scholars consider this to be a rather obvious intrusion of later Christian attitudes towards Judaism, but if this is true, it is surprising that John has Jesus affirming in the next sentence that 'scripture cannot be annulled' – a possible parallel to the 'not one stroke of the law' saying. Perhaps we are to understand 'your law' to mean 'your interpretation of Scripture', similar to the way that the Synoptic Gospels portray Jesus as criticizing the Pharisees for putting their 'traditions' above Scripture.

Second, the gist of the argument appears to be: Why do you object to me calling myself 'Son of God' when Scripture applies the term 'gods' to all who have received the 'word of God'? Indeed, if we read the second half of the quoted verse, it goes on to say that they are also called 'sons of the most high' (NIV). Rudolf Bultmann was of the opinion that this is not put forward as a serious argument but is simply playing the rabbis at their own game.[4] But Anthony Hanson has countered this by noting that in rabbinic tradition, Psalm 82 was associated with the giving of the law at Mount Sinai.[5] He thinks that Jesus is drawing on this background to argue that if the word of God gave its recipients a quasi-divine status, how much more is it applicable to the one who is the Word incarnate (John 1.14)? Nevertheless, as with the 'bread of life' quotation, few scholars believe that we are dealing with something that Jesus actually said.

John 13.18–20

All four Gospels record a final meal with his disciples at which Jesus predicts betrayal by Judas. Matthew and Mark are almost identical (Matt. 26.20–25; Mark 14.17–21), with an opening statement ('Truly I tell you, one of you will betray me'), the disciples' bewilderment ('They began to be distressed and say to him one after another, "Surely, not I?"'), a further assertion that it would be one of those present ('one who is dipping bread into the bowl with me') and then a word of judgement ('woe to that one by whom the Son of Man is betrayed!'). The expression that Jesus uses of the betrayer ('dipping bread into the bowl with me') emphasizes the intimacy that currently exists between them but is about to be broken. However, some scholars have suggested that the words might have been chosen to allude to David's complaint in Psalm 41.9 that in the midst of his troubles, even his trusted friend, who ate bread with him, has now renounced him:

> All who hate me whisper together about me; they imagine the worst for me. They think that a deadly thing has fastened on me, that I will not rise again from where I lie. Even my bosom friend in whom I trusted, who ate of my bread, has lifted [lit. magnified] the heel against me. (Ps. 41.7–9)

With this in mind, what is interesting about John's account is that this text is specifically quoted ('But it is to fulfil the scripture') in the form 'The one who ate my bread has lifted his heel against me' (John 13.18). The text appears to be a translation from the Hebrew since the LXX has a different reading for the last phrase ('by craftiness' rather than 'the heel').[6] Whether John knew any of the Synoptic Gospels and is consciously making the allusion more explicit remains a matter of debate. This same question also applies to the identification of the betrayer with Judas. In the Synoptic Gospels there is no direct identification, but in John 13.26 Jesus says 'It is the one to whom I give this piece of bread when I have dipped it in the dish', and then specifically offers it to Judas with the words 'Do quickly what you are going to do' (John 13.27).

The majority of scholars believe that this is a later rationalization of the story, demonstrating that the betrayal was to fulfil Scripture, rather than Jesus being 'outwitted' by Judas' treachery. Nevertheless, if it was 'obvious' to John that the reference to 'dipping bread' was an allusion to Psalm 41.9, it might suggest that it was obvious to Matthew and Mark also, which is why they did not feel the need to add an explicit quotation. If this is the case, then we have another text that Jesus applies to some aspect of his enemies. Thus while it is unlikely that Jesus explicitly quoted Psalm 41.9 (as John states), it could be used as supporting evidence that behind all the accounts is a genuine allusion by Jesus to the psalm. Faced with a betrayal from one of his own disciples, Jesus thought of David's plight when even his 'bosom friend' turned against him.

John 15.25

As with the quotation in John 10.34, Jesus introduces the words 'They hated me without a cause' with a phrase (*'their* law') that seems to distance himself from Scripture (see also John 8.17). The text comes at the end of a section where Jesus explains that the world will hate the disciples just as it has hated him. The actual quotation only consists of three Greek words (*emisesan me dorean*), so there is some uncertainty about tracing its source. The most likely suggestion is Psalm 69.4 ('More in number than the hairs of my head are those who *hate me without cause*; many are those who would destroy me, my enemies who accuse me falsely'), especially as this psalm is quoted several times in the New Testament. On the other hand, it is precisely because the early Church believed that Psalm 69 was about Jesus (Acts 1.20; Rom. 11.9–10) that scholars question whether it was actually spoken by Jesus here in John, especially as it does not occur in any of the other Gospels. The general picture that Jesus thought of the plight of David when contemplating his own fate is plausible and coheres with the Synoptic Gospels, but it is unlikely that Jesus said these precise words.

Allusions

In the dialogue with Nathaniel, where Jesus calls him an 'Israelite in whom there is no deceit' (John 1.47), the final saying is: 'Very truly, I tell you, you will see heaven opened and the angels of God ascending and descending upon the Son of Man' (John 1.51). This somewhat obscure promise is reminiscent of Jacob's dream in Genesis 28.12–15, where he sees a 'ladder set up on the earth, the top of it reaching to heaven; and the angels of God were ascending and descending on it' (Gen. 28.12). In common with Jewish interpretation, the fact that the final pronoun ('descending on *it*') is unspecified means that it could be read as 'descending on him', and this appears to be the catalyst for further specifying it as the 'Son of Man'. Though the quotation is obscure and its fulfilment does not appear anywhere in John's Gospel, there is a certain appropriateness to Nathaniel, a true Israelite, since Jacob's name was later changed to 'Israel' (Gen. 32.28).

In John's account of the cleansing of the temple, Jesus does not utter the words of Isaiah 56.7/Jeremiah 7.11 ('My house shall be a house of prayer; but you have made it a den of robbers'), but says to those selling doves: 'Take these things out of here! Stop making my Father's house a market-place' (John 2.16). Although most scholars think that John is responsible for placing this incident at the beginning of Jesus' ministry rather than at its end, the accusation of making the temple a marketplace seems more appropriate to the situation than the Synoptic reference to a 'house of prayer' or a 'den of robbers'. Indeed, it has been suggested that the words could be an allusion to Zechariah 14.21, which promises that 'there shall no longer be traders[7] in the house of the LORD of hosts on that day' (Zech. 14.21). Perhaps the most we can say is that at some point in his ministry, Jesus launched a protest against the running of the temple and justified it by reference to Scripture, although there is some ambiguity as to which Scriptures were actually cited.

In his reply to Nicodemus, Jesus states that there is earthly knowledge and heavenly knowledge, and in words reminiscent of John 1.51, 'No one has ascended into heaven except the one descended from heaven, the Son of Man' (John 3.13). He then gives an illustration of both his fate and his role in salvation: 'And just as Moses lifted up the serpent in the wilderness, so must the Son of Man be lifted up, that whoever believes in him may have eternal life' (John 3.14–15). The incident to which this refers occurs in Numbers 21.1–9, where Moses is told to make a bronze serpent on a pole, so that those who have been bitten by a serpent can look at it and be healed. This use of Scripture is often called 'typology', where certain events or people are said to correspond to later events. In this case, the lifting up of the serpent on to the pole (though 'lifting' is not specifically stated in Numbers) corresponds with the crucifixion (and possibly the ascension, since Jesus has been talking about ascent and descent from heaven), while looking to the serpent for healing corresponds to believing in the Son of Man to gain eternal life. The fact that the allusion is closely tied with receiving 'eternal life', John's characteristic way of referring to salvation (and very different from the Synoptic Gospels), leads most scholars to conclude that these are the words of John, not Jesus.

In the course of a heated dispute with 'the Jews', Jesus initiates a debate about Abraham and his true heirs: 'If you were Abraham's children, you would be doing what Abraham did' (John 8.39). He then accuses them of plotting murder, demonstrating that they are children of the devil rather than children of Abraham. They respond by accusing him of having a demon, which leads to this climactic exchange:

> 'Your ancestor Abraham rejoiced that he would see my day; he saw it and was glad.' Then the Jews said to him, 'You are not yet fifty years old, and have you seen Abraham?' Jesus said to them, 'Very truly, I tell you, before Abraham was, I am.' (John 8.56–58)

There is a Q saying where John the Baptist challenges the Jews for thinking that their Abrahamic ancestry will save them from the wrath to come (Matt. 3.9/Luke 3.8). There is also a Q saying where Jesus speaks of a heavenly feast in the company of Abraham, Isaac and Jacob (Matt. 8.11/Luke 13.28), and a number of references in Luke's Gospel to people being children of Abraham (Luke 13.16; 19.9). It is therefore quite plausible that Jesus challenged reliance on Abrahamic ancestry, but the explicit reference to pre-existence ('before Abraham was, I am') appears to be another example of John's theology, especially if the 'I am' is intended as a reference to the divine name in Exodus 3.14 ('Thus you shall say to the Israelites, "I AM has sent me to you"').

We have already mentioned the explicit quotation of Psalm 82.6 in John 10.34, but we will now consider the use of the shepherd and sheep imagery in that chapter. In the Synoptic Gospels, Jesus describes a crowd of people as being 'like sheep without a shepherd' (Mark 6.34), tells a parable about a shepherd going in search of his lost sheep (Matt. 18.12) and uses Zechariah 13.7 to predict the striking of the shepherd and the scattering of the sheep. Here in John 10, Jesus castigates shepherds who do not protect their sheep (v. 12) and refers to himself as the 'good shepherd' who 'lays down his life for the sheep' (v. 11). As in the Synoptic parable, the shepherd must go looking for the sheep ('I have other sheep that do not belong to this fold. I must bring them also' – v. 16), but there are two features of John 10 that are not found in the Synoptic Gospels.

The first is the idea that the sheep know the shepherd and respond to his voice. This is said to parallel the way God and Jesus know one another ('I know my own and my own know me, just as the Father knows me and I know the Father' – John 10.14–15). The second is the idea that Jesus gathers the sheep so that there might be 'one flock, one shepherd' (v. 16). Both sayings reflect features of John's theology, but many of the ideas can also be found in Ezekiel 34, where God first castigates self-serving shepherds (Ezek. 34.1–10) and then asserts that he will be Israel's shepherd, seeking them out from foreign lands and bringing them back to their own land (Ezek. 34.11–16). Somewhat surprisingly, the passage then goes on to say that God will establish a shepherd over Israel, and calls him 'my servant David' (Ezek. 34.23). Since King David is long dead, this can only mean that one day there will be a royal figure who will shepherd Israel – it is easy to see how the early Church would identify this with Jesus.

Jesus as shepherd

Though the specific claim to being the 'good shepherd' is unique to John, it is worth asking if there is sufficient evidence from the Synoptic Gospels as to whether Jesus saw himself as the promised shepherd of Ezekiel 34. In favour are the following passages: Mark 6.34, where Jesus describes the hungry crowd as 'like sheep without a shepherd', and goes on to feed them; Matthew 10.6, where Jesus instructs the disciples to go 'to the lost sheep of the house of Israel', a task that is clearly part of Jesus' overall mission; and Matthew 15.24, where Jesus describes his own mission with the words: 'I was sent only to the lost sheep of the house of Israel'. The first could simply be a metaphor, but the reference to the 'house of Israel' in the last two verses points back to Israel's history. Tom Wright is one scholar who finds this significant, claiming that Jesus 'invoked the image of the shepherd . . . with roots deep in the ancient Israelite traditions of monarchy, but one that also spoke of YHWH himself as the shepherd of his people, taking over from the false shepherds who had been feeding themselves instead of the sheep, and (in several of the relevant passages) thereby bringing about the true homecoming, the moment of covenant renewal'.[8]

King of the Jews

All four Gospels state that Jesus was crucified as 'king of the Jews' and that an inscription was placed on the cross to that effect. It is the central feature of Pilate's interrogation (Matt. 27.11; Mark 15.2; Luke 23.3; John 18.33), the mockery of the soldiers (Matt. 27.29; Mark 15.18; John 19.3) and the mockery of those witnessing the crucifixion (Matt. 27.42; Mark 15.32; Luke 23.38). The inscription reads either: 'The King of the Jews' (Mark 15.26); 'This is the King of the Jews' (Luke 23.38); 'This is Jesus, the King of the Jews' (Matt. 27.37); or 'Jesus of Nazareth, King of the Jews' (John 19.19). In addition, John adds an exchange between Pilate and the Jews over the wording of the inscription:

> Pilate also had an inscription written and put on the cross. It read, 'Jesus of Nazareth, the King of the Jews.' Many of the Jews read this inscription, because the place where Jesus was crucified was near the city; and it was written in Hebrew, in Latin, and in Greek. Then the chief priests of the Jews said to Pilate, 'Do not write, "The King of the Jews", but, "This man said, I am King of the Jews."' Pilate answered, 'What I have written I have written.' (John 19.19–22)

The variation in the wording could be taken as evidence that as no one knew what the inscription said, each Gospel writer offered his best guess. On the other hand, they all agree that it said something about Jesus being 'king of the Jews', and John seems to think it was well known that Jesus had made such a claim. Whether or not that is the case, it is Pilate's official verdict, and it seems reasonable to conclude that Jesus' actions and teaching led *some* to think that this was what he was claiming, whether he did so explicitly or not.

References to Scripture

In a speech that begins with the accusation that Jesus should not have healed on the Sabbath (John 5.16), Jesus ends by saying: 'You search the scriptures because you think that in them you have eternal life; and it is they that testify on my behalf' (John 5.39). This is then narrowed down to a statement about the law: 'If you believed Moses, you would believe me, for he wrote about me' (John 5.46). This is close to the words at the end of Luke's Gospel and raises similar doubts, for Jesus asserts that the Jews searched the Scriptures in order to find 'eternal life'. Since this is John's characteristic way of referring to salvation (21 times), it is likely to have originated with him.

As in the healing story in John 5, the issue in John 7.19–24 is also concerned with Jesus healing on a Sabbath, but there is an original element to the argument. Jesus asserts that Moses gave them circumcision and so circumcision is performed on the Sabbath, in order that the law of Moses may not be broken (John 7.22–23). However, it is clear from Genesis 17 that it was Abraham who gave them circumcision, and the author of the Gospel feels the need to point this out in a parenthesis ('it is, of course, not from Moses, but from the patriarchs'). This could be taken as evidence of authenticity, for it is unlikely that the author would invent a saying he then immediately has to correct (criterion of embarrassment). Though the specific discussion is open to question (it is once again in the service of John's theology), it might be seen as additional evidence that Jesus upheld the law but differed in some of his interpretations, notably what can and cannot be done on the Sabbath.

Conclusion

Since John is so different from the Synoptic Gospels and its theology of pre-existence, divinity and eternal life pervades the whole Gospel, most scholars do not think it has much to offer in determining what Jesus actually said, even though its theological reflections have had a profound influence on the beliefs of the Church. However, it might provide corroborating evidence that Jesus identified himself with Israel's shepherd, that he acted in such a way that it was taken as a claim to be the King of the Jews, and that he thought of David's plight in Psalm 41 when he contemplated rejection by a trusted friend.

John shares with the Synoptic Gospels the view that Jesus upheld the law, while debating such matters as what can or cannot be done on the Sabbath. The differences in the latter example are instructive. In the Synoptic Gospels, Jesus justifies his actions by asserting that it is better to do good than to do bad on the Sabbath. In John's Gospel the argument is more Christological; God is at work doing good on the Sabbath, so Jesus must be also (John 5.17). Few scholars think Jesus used such an argument (it is the opposite of the criterion of embarrassment – it serves John's purpose), but it supports the general picture from the Synoptic Gospels – Jesus claimed to uphold the law while engaging in disputes over what can or cannot be done on the Sabbath.

5

Jesus and Scripture – minimalist views

Introduction

During the nineteenth century the traditional view – at least since Augustine – that Matthew was the earliest Gospel was replaced by the view that Mark was the earliest and was used by Matthew and Luke as one of their sources. The implications of this hypothesis (Markan priority) were enormous, for many of the texts used to support traditional Christian doctrines came from either Matthew (Jesus as founder of the Church) or John (Jesus as the incarnation of God). Influenced by the growing status of Darwinian evolution, the idea that the traditions about Jesus developed and expanded was persuasive. One only has to look at the formula agreed at the Council at Chalcedon (451 CE) to realize the extent of doctrinal development in the Church's understanding of Jesus. Despite what it claims (see italics), this is hardly what the historical Jesus said to his followers:

> Therefore, following the holy Fathers, we all with one accord teach men to acknowledge one and the same Son, our Lord Jesus Christ, at once complete in Godhead and complete in manhood, truly God and truly man, consisting also of a reasonable soul and body; of one substance with the Father as regards his Godhead, and at the same time of one substance with us as regards his manhood; like us in all respects, apart from sin; as regards his Godhead, begotten of the Father before the ages, but yet as regards his manhood begotten, for us men and for our salvation, of Mary the Virgin, the God-bearer; one and the same Christ, Son, Lord, Only-begotten, recognized in two natures, without confusion, without change, without division, without separation; the distinction of natures being in no way annulled by the union, but rather the characteristics of each nature being preserved and coming together to form one person and subsistence, not as parted or separated into two persons, but one and the same Son and Only-begotten God the Word, Lord Jesus Christ; even as the prophets from earliest times spoke of him, *and our Lord Jesus Christ himself taught us*, and the creed of the Fathers has handed down to us.[1]

For some scholars, such developments were seen as evidence for the reliability of Mark's Gospel. For example, it is clear that Mark believed that Jesus was the Son of God (Mark 1.1; 1.11; 9.7; 15.39), but he does not present Jesus as claiming this for himself. He also believed that Jesus was the Jewish Messiah (Mark 14.62), but nowhere in the Gospel does Jesus openly proclaim it. Indeed, the Jesus of Mark's Gospel is an ambiguous figure, a far cry from the doctrinal statements of Chalcedon, and thus likely to be authentic. When combined with the Q hypothesis, many scholars believe that there is a solid foundation on which to build, even if the evidence from the later Gospels must be handled with care.

However, at the beginning of the twentieth century the German scholar William Wrede challenged the view that the ambiguities and oddities of Mark's Gospel are signs of authenticity. He sought to reveal as fabrication Mark's picture of Jesus as someone who knew he was Messiah and Son of God but wished to keep his identity quiet. For Wrede, it simply did not ring true that someone who miraculously feeds crowds of 5,000 and 4,000 would wish to keep his identity secret.[2] The superficiality of the position can be seen in Mark's story of the little girl brought back to life. Jesus came to the house and saw a crowd of people weeping and wailing over her death (Mark 5.38). He then entered the house, brought the girl back to life and ordered the parents not to let anyone know about it (Mark 5.43). But the house is surrounded by mourners – how could they possibly hope to keep it quiet or indeed want to? Such a command is not only unrealistic but unkind to the parents. It was clearly problematic for Matthew, who omits the command to silence and thus gives the story a very different outcome:

> When Jesus came to the leader's house and saw the flute-players and the crowd making a commotion, he said, 'Go away; for the girl is not dead but sleeping.' And they laughed at him. But when the crowd had been put outside, he went in and took her by the hand, and the girl got up. And the report of this spread throughout that district.[3]
>
> (Matt. 9.23–26)

Geza Vermes

A more recent example of a minimalist view is the Jewish scholar, Geza Vermes. In his book *Jesus the Jew*, published in 1973,[4] Vermes sought to locate Jesus' teaching within the Judaism of his day rather than later Christianity. He focused on the four titles bestowed on Jesus that are prominent in Christian tradition, namely Jesus as Lord, Messiah, Son of Man and Son of God, and explores what these would have meant if uttered in Jesus' mother tongue (Aramaic). For the first two, he notes the ambiguity that Mark presents both titles in his Gospel. Jesus asks the scribes how they can say that the Messiah is the son of David when David (citing Psalm 110.1) calls him Lord. There is no suggestion that Jesus is applying this to himself, and in fact this type of textual 'hair-splitting' is more characteristic of the early Church than it is of Jesus' teaching (Gal. 3.16; Heb. 7.2). Furthermore, Acts 2.34–35 applies Psalm 110.1 to Jesus because he rose from the dead and is now seated at God's right hand, while Hebrews 5.6 applies Psalm 110.4 to Jesus because he is high priest of a different order from the Levitical priesthood. Vermes concludes that it is unlikely that the dialogue about the meaning of Psalm 110.1 goes back to Jesus; it was only of interest to the later Church.

In Peter's confession ('You are the Messiah'), Mark has Jesus ignore the affirmation and declare that the 'Son of Man must undergo great suffering' (8.31). When Peter finds this difficult to accept, Jesus rebukes him for setting his mind on human rather than divine things. He even suggests that such a view comes from the devil ('Get behind me Satan!') rather than God or the Scriptures. Most scholars agree that Mark thinks that Jesus rejected all ideas of a militant Messiah, but whereas traditionalists conclude that this is because Jesus saw himself as a *suffering* Messiah, Vermes concludes that Jesus did not see himself as the Messiah at all. After all, the traditional passages about the Messiah (Ps. 2.8–9; Isa. 11.4) are about the establishment of kingship and the conquest of enemies. If Jesus rejected such a role, then he did not see himself as the Jewish Messiah.

What this passage does indicate is that Jesus preferred to speak in terms of 'Son of Man' rather than Messiah. But what would this phrase have meant when spoken in Aramaic? In a complex linguistic chapter, Vermes argues that the majority of the sayings would have been heard as an oblique reference to himself, 'the man', as we might say. Thus instead of saying such things as 'I have authority to forgive sins' or 'I am lord of the Sabbath', Jesus uses an idiom that would have sounded something like 'The man has authority to forgive sins' or 'The man is lord of the Sabbath', meaning himself. It was only when such sayings were translated into Greek that they were heard as a specific title ('The Son of Man has authority to forgive sins').

However, there are two instances where 'the man' is connected with 'clouds of heaven' (Mark 13.26; 14.62), which clearly suggests a reference to Daniel 7.13. For Vermes, these are rather obvious attempts by Mark to portray Jesus as predicting a second coming, a view that is not only foreign to the rest of the Gospel but also contrary to the Daniel passage, where the human figure comes 'to God' not 'from God'. One might also note that it is somewhat illogical to argue that Jesus distanced himself from notions of conquest and power ('the Son of Man came not to be served but to serve' – Mark 10.45), only to state that this is how it will be in his second coming. If the idea of gaining followers through conquest is unethical, how does it become acceptable at the second coming?

Concerning the authenticity of the title 'Son of God', the heavenly voice at Jesus' baptism and transfiguration declares that Jesus is God's son, but the only saying in Mark where Jesus makes such a claim is Mark 13.32: 'But about that day or hour no one knows, neither the angels in heaven, nor the Son, but only the Father.' The fact that Jesus is here admitting ignorance of something has been a strong argument for its authenticity (criterion of embarrassment). Who would invent such a saying? But Vermes notes that it is part of the same apocalyptic discourse as the 'clouds of heaven' saying (Mark 13.26), and thus probably comes from the same source. Jesus did not claim to be *the* 'Son of God'.

In *The Authentic Gospel of Jesus*, published 30 years after *Jesus the Jew*, Vermes looks at Jesus' use of Scripture more systematically. He notes that compared with New Testament writers like Paul, Jesus' use of Scripture is 'relatively rare'.[5] He then considers 41 examples, which he divides into four categories. The first is Mark, the earliest Gospel, which contains 19 examples. Vermes only regards four of these as authentic (prohibition of divorce, keeping the commandments, the question about the first commandment and the forsaken saying). The second category is Q, the material common to Matthew and Luke but absent from Mark. This source, if it existed, is usually dated a decade or so earlier than Mark and is therefore very important. Vermes finds 11 examples in Q, of which four are regarded as authentic (retaliation forbidden, love of neighbour, the golden rule – 'do to others as you would have them do to you' – and Jesus' reply to John the Baptist). The third is the material unique to Matthew (usually designated as M), of which there are seven examples, three of which Vermes regards as authentic (prohibition of murder, adultery and swearing falsely). The fourth is the material unique to Luke (L), and Vermes regards none of the four examples (Nazareth sermon, counted among the lawless, comfort for the daughters of Jerusalem and commending his spirit to God) as authentic.

Of the eleven examples that he does accept as authentic, nine are to do with the law, either citing the commandments (Mark 10.19; 12.29–31) or deepening the commandments – as with the prohibition of divorce (Mark 10.11–12) or the antitheses in the Sermon on the Mount ('You have heard . . . but I say unto you'). The only two that are not concerned with the law are the forsaken saying on the cross (Mark 15.34) and Jesus' reply to the messengers of John the Baptist (Matt. 11.4–6/Luke 7.22–23). In the latter, Jesus responds to John's question ('Are you the one who is to come, or are we to wait for another?') by citing a string of phrases from Isaiah (Isa. 29.18; 35.5–6; 61.1) that allude to the messianic age ('the blind receive their sight, the lame walk, the lepers are cleansed, the deaf hear, the dead are raised, the poor have good news brought to them'). One might conclude from this that Jesus was claiming to be the Messiah, especially as Vermes himself cites a text from the Dead Sea Scrolls where such an identification is made: '[the hea]vens and the earth will listen to his Messiah . . . He who liberates the captives, restores sight to the blind, straightens the b[ent] . . . He will heal the wounded, and revive the dead and bring good news to the poor' (*Messianic Apocalypse*, 4Q521). However, Vermes does not think that such a claim is compatible with the overall picture of Jesus that has emerged from his analysis – Jesus directed people to God and his kingdom rather than drawing attention to himself. Thus Vermes acknowledges that the healings and exorcisms are 'part of the general Jewish belief surrounding the advent of the reign of God' and 'indicators of the nearness or presence of the Kingdom', but does not think that Jesus cited them as 'evidence of personal greatness'.[6]

One of Vermes's main arguments is that Christian interpretation of the Gospels has operated with a highly distorted understanding of first-century Judaism. This takes two forms. Positively, it assumes that ideas such as the coming 'son of man' and the 'suffering servant' were so well known that the merest allusion would be sufficient to evoke them. Thus in the mid-twentieth century it was common to argue that Jesus applied Isaiah 53 to his first coming (victory through suffering), and Daniel 7 (receiving an eternal kingdom) to his second coming.[7] But advances in scholarship during the twentieth century have shown that the Jews were not looking for a 'suffering servant', and the idiom of 'son of man' was simply a reference to humanity in general, perhaps with a self-reference. Operating in Galilee and speaking in Aramaic, it is hard to see how any of Jesus' listeners would have deduced that he was claiming to be *the* suffering servant or *the* Son of Man, since these were not recognized titles.

Negatively, the bitter disputes between the early Church and the Jews indicated in the New Testament (Acts 8.1; 1 Thess. 2.14–16), and followed by centuries of antagonism, have led to the common view that the Pharisees were self-righteous legalists who believed that salvation would only come to those who kept every detail of the(ir) law. But deriving our view of Judaism from literature that is hostile to it is fallacious. If we want to know what the Pharisees believed, we need to consult either contemporary writers such as Philo and Josephus, contemporary documents such as the Dead Sea Scrolls or the codification of traditions found in *Jewish* documents, such as the Mishnah and Tosefta. And these offer a very different picture of the Pharisees from what we find in the Gospels.

For example, in the debate about Corban, Mark has Jesus condemning the Pharisees because they use this legal loophole to defraud their parents and thus break the commandment to honour one's mother and father. But we know from both the Dead Sea Scrolls and the Mishnah that a ruling had already been given on this question. If there is a conflict between a vow made to God and honouring one's parents, it is the commandment that takes priority. Vermes concludes that the 'Gospel picture of the Pharisees' stance is not just exaggerated; it is unmistakably a caricature'.[8] Thus when in the same incident Mark has Jesus quoting Isaiah 29.13 in its Septuagintal form ('teaching human precepts as doctrines') instead of its Hebrew form ('their worship of me is a human commandment learned by rote'), we are unquestionably hearing the voice of later Church disputes.

If Vermes is correct that 30 of the 41 sayings (73 per cent) concerning Jesus' use of Scripture come from the early Church, we might reasonably ask whether it is possible to say anything at all about Jesus. It looks as though the tradition has become so distorted that the original Jesus has been lost forever. Vermes does not conclude this, and in his final chapter and epilogue offers a sketch of what he calls 'the authentic gospel of Jesus'. He begins by stating three points about Jesus that he believes his studies have established:

1 Jesus' mission was to his fellow Jews, to whom the kingdom belonged. Any concern for non-Jews, such as the Syrophoenician woman (Mark 7.24–30), was the exception rather than the rule.
2 The kingdom was imminent, as indicated by his charismatic ministry of healings and exorcisms and gave an 'eschatological urgency' to his preaching. His message of faith and repentance was to prepare for the coming kingdom.
3 He expected this to come in his lifetime and was despondent ('why have you forsaken me?') when this did not happen. The ideas that his death was a sacrifice for sins, his resurrection a conquest of death and his second coming an eternal reign are all attempts by the early Church to find some significance in this tragedy. They were not part of Jesus' message.[9]

Vermes thinks that the best description of Jesus is a *hasid*, a latter-day prophet and mystic who believed that the 'day of the Lord' was imminent. It is this belief that shaped his radical view of the law: 'Seen through the prism of Jesus' piety, the purpose of the Law was not simply the regulation of everyday life and religious practice; it was above all intended to teach Jews the duty of obedience and total self-surrender to God.'[10] Jesus was not an *interpreter* of the law as such, but wished to confront his fellow Jews with the need for total loyalty to God in the light of the coming kingdom. And while Jesus did believe that the signs prophesied by Isaiah were being fulfilled in his healings and exorcisms, he did not conclude from this that he was the Messiah. They were evidence that God was working through him and that the new age was dawning, but not that he himself was the one who would bring this about.

John Dominic Crossan

One of the puzzling things about Vermes's reconstruction is that Jesus is said to believe that the kingdom belonged to the Jews and was coming in his lifetime, but only made a single reference (the reply to John the Baptist) to Israel's prophets. Crossan solves this puzzle by suggesting that while Jesus initially favoured the sort of restoration programme preached by John the Baptist, he later turned away from it and developed his own message. This is the background to the Q saying (Matt. 11.11/Luke 7.28) that despite the fact that John was the greatest of the prophets, even the least person in God's kingdom is greater than John. According to Crossan, Jesus' mission was emphatically *not* directed towards preparing the Jews for the coming 'day of the Lord', but was a present reality, aimed at the downtrodden and dispossessed. It was a 'religious and economic egalitarianism that negated alike and at once the hierarchical and patronal normalcies of Jewish religion and Roman power'.[11]

Crossan makes rigorous use of the criterion of multiple attestation by demanding that authentic sayings be attested by two or more independent sources. The key word here is independent. All of Mark's scriptural material is found in Matthew, but that is not an independent witness, for Matthew took it from Mark. It would only be regarded as authentic if it is also found in an independent source, such as Q, M or L. This also rules out material that occurs in Matthew and Luke but is not in Mark, such as the reply to John the Baptist, for they both took it from Q and it is therefore only singly attested. Thus the question we posed to Vermes (if the tradition is as corrupt as this, can we say anything at all about Jesus?) is even more pertinent to Crossan. With the bar placed as high as this, can anything survive?

The answer is yes, and that is because Crossan thinks that other works, such as the *Didache* and the *Gospel of Thomas*, contain traditions as early as Mark and Q. Thus if a saying is in Mark and *Gospel of Thomas* or Q and *Gospel of Thomas*, it is doubly attested because Crossan considers *Gospel of Thomas* to be independent of the canonical Gospels. That is why he accepts the saying about being greater than John the Baptist in Matthew 11.11/Luke 7.28 (Q); there is also a version of it in *Gospel of Thomas* 46 ('whoever among you becomes a child will know the kingdom, and will become greater than John'). It should be pointed out that Crossan does not accept that everything in these other works is early; like the canonical Gospels, they have also been subject to embellishment. Indeed, following the work of John Kloppenborg,[12] he thinks that Q was also subject to embellishment, and so criteria are needed to distinguish early traditions from the later embellishments. But they allow Crossan to compile a database of 131 sayings that he thinks belong to the earliest layer of traditions (30–60 CE) and have multiple attestation.

Gospel of Thomas

When the Coptic version of the *Gospel of Thomas* was discovered in 1945 (some Greek fragments had been found earlier), most scholars concluded that it was a second-century distortion of the canonical Gospels. Among its 114 sayings, said to have been given to Thomas secretly by Jesus, there are certainly some very odd ones, such as Jesus' comment about Mary: 'Behold, I shall guide her to make her male, so that she too may become a living spirit resembling you males. For every female who makes herself male will enter the kingdom of heaven' (114). But there are also a number of sayings that look more primitive than the corresponding texts in the canonical Gospels. For example, the parable of the four soils lacks the allegorical explanation found in the Synoptic Gospels, and the parable of the 'wheat and tares' is less than half the length of Matthew's version. According to Helmut Koester, of the 79 sayings that *Gospel of Thomas* has in common with the Synoptic Gospels, 46 belong to Q, a text usually dated a decade earlier than Mark. This is why Crossan and others believe that *Gospel of Thomas* is a valuable source

---

Crossan entitles his book, published in 1991, *The Historical Jesus: The Life of a Mediterranean Jewish Peasant*, and the word 'peasant' is important. The Gospel portrait of Jesus debating the finer points of law with scribes and Pharisees does not belong to the early multiply attested material. Jesus was a peasant from a backwater village and most likely illiterate. His teaching is not characterized by learned exegesis or even prophetic discernment, but pithy aphorisms that turn many of society's 'norms' on their head (turn the other cheek/ blessed are the poor). The parables he tells are witty and subversive (invite the poor and blind to your dinner parties) rather than religious allegories about God and his vineyard or shepherding his sheep. In the first half of his book, Crossan surveys a number of first-century figures and concludes that Jesus comes closest to the wandering Cynic philosophers who sharply criticized those in authority and advocated a life of simple self-sufficiency.[14] The difference is that Jesus was a *Jewish* peasant and did not preach self-sufficiency like the Cynics, but rather communal interdependence.

This is demonstrated in the two facets of Jesus' ministry, which Crossan labels 'magic and meals'. By 'magic' he is not suggesting that Jesus was a charlatan but that he 'magically' took sick outcasts and reconnected them with their communities (he is agnostic as to whether the sick person's symptoms actually disappeared). This was 'acted out' in his practice of eating with 'sinners and tax-collectors'. Politics and social custom dictate who can eat with whom. Likewise with religious rules about purity. But Jesus' practice of eating with anybody subverted both political and religious sensibilities, and his teaching that shared meals are a parable of the kingdom of God encouraged all to believe that they could experience God outside the 'rules'. This is illustrated by the sayings that compare the kingdom of God with becoming like a child. The earliest source is *Gospel of Thomas* 22, which puts it starkly: 'Jesus saw infants being suckled. He said to his disciples, "These infants being suckled are like those who enter the kingdom."'[15] This is not about humility, as Mark 10.13–16 implies and Matthew 18.1–4 states explicitly, and certainly not about spiritual rebirth, as John 3.1–10 presents it. Being a child was to be a 'nobody, with the possibility of becoming a somebody absolutely dependent on parental discretion'.[16] According to Crossan, Jesus' message of the kingdom was an invitation to those who were considered 'nobodies' by the elite. It had nothing to do with fulfilling scriptural promises about reigning as king over an elect people and bringing about the end of the world. These are the fantasies of the early Church, which has completely misunderstood the message and mission of their so-called founder.

Marcus Borg

Marcus Borg is often considered as a 'bridge' figure. He shares with Vermes the idea that Jesus was a mystic or holy man (his term is 'Spirit-person') and that his mission was directed towards Israel. On the other hand, he agrees with Crossan that Jesus was an intensely 'political' figure (like Israel's classical prophets) as well as a dispenser of subversive wisdom (his term is 'sage'). In agreement with both, he denies that Jesus spoke about an apocalyptic end to the world, used 'Son of Man' as a title, saw himself as the 'suffering servant' or claimed to be the Messiah. However, in his first book, *Conflict, Holiness, and Politics in the Teachings of Jesus*, published in 1984, he does accept the authenticity of the following: the appeal to David in the cornfields incident (Mark 2.25); the application of Isaiah 29.13 to the Pharisees (Mark 7.6–7); his entry into Jerusalem on a donkey as an 'acted fulfilment' of Zechariah 9.9 (Mark 11.1–11); the words of Isaiah 56.7/ Jeremiah 7.11 against the guardians of the temple (Mark 11.17) and the parable of the vineyard as a critique of Israel's hierarchy (Mark 12.1–9):

> Thus, like the classical prophets of the Hebrew Bible, Jesus sought to divert his people from a course which was leading to catastrophe. Apparently knowing that the likely outcome would be his death, he went to Jerusalem during the season of Passover, there to make one final dramatic appeal to his people at the center of their corporate life.[17]

We will confine ourselves to his treatment of the cornfields incident, the words against the temple authorities and the parable of the vineyard. Beginning with the cornfields incident, we have noted how Jesus' appeal to David eating the consecrated bread has puzzled commentators. Borg suggests the meaning hinges on two parallels. The first is that both are concerned with regulations intended to safeguard that which is holy. The second is that both are on an urgent mission where the fate of Israel is at stake. David was remembered, Borg says, as the 'nation-builder and Temple-planner', and so a danger to him was a danger to the future of Israel. Similarly, the fact that Jesus and the disciples were walking among cornfields on the Sabbath instead of being at home with their families implies that they were on a mission: 'The incident may thus suggest that Jesus believed that a state of emergency existed for Israel, and, moreover, that the activity of him and his disciples was organically connected to the resolution of the crisis.'[18] For Borg, it is a question of hermeneutics. Is the law to be interpreted within a holiness paradigm based on separation or a compassion paradigm based on mercy? The Pharisees advocated the former, but Jesus advocated compassion, as can be seen from the other Sabbath controversies: they regularly untie their animals on the Sabbath (Luke 13.15–16); they immediately rescue a son or ox if he/it has fallen into a pit (Luke 14.5); they immediately rescue a sheep if it has fallen into a pit (Matt. 12.11–12). Thus 'the sabbath was a

day for works of compassion . . . [and] as the core value for interpreting the Torah stretched and at times burst the boundaries set by the
quest for holiness.'[19]

Along with most scholars, Borg sees Jesus' action in the temple as
a symbolic or prophetic act rather than an actual attempt to clear it,
which would have required an army. Such acts usually take a threefold
form: the act is performed; a question is asked; its meaning is
explained. Thus it is likely that the story was transmitted with an
explanation of its meaning, so that the burden of proof lies with
those who deny that Isaiah 56.7/Jeremiah 7.11 is that explanation.
As to the meaning of the words, Borg begins with Jeremiah 7.11 and
argues that the Greek *lestai* means 'brigands' rather than the traditional 'robbers'. Jesus is not accusing the money-changers of exploitation since 'there is little evidence that inflated prices were charged
or that pilgrims were fleeced'.[20] Rather, the charge is violent conduct.
Here we must note an important modification in Borg's thought. In
the original 1984 edition of his book, Borg suggests that this violent
conduct is associated with the temple's role as a focus of nationalist
resistance to Rome. In his introduction to the 1998 edition, however,
he has changed his mind on this issue and now thinks it is to do with
the temple's role in supporting what he calls a domination system:
'Rather than it being a center of justice for widows and orphans,
it has become the den of the elites who pillaged the populace.'[21] This
is also the point of quoting Isaiah 56.7, which emphasizes inclusion.
The temple was to be a house of prayer for the nations, not the head-
quarters of a domination system that keeps people in submission.

His discussion of the vineyard parable comes in his analysis of
what he calls the 'threat tradition'. Of the 32 examples with an
'identifiable content', 9 exhibit a 'taken away/given to others' pattern,
11 speak of destruction in historical terms and 12 speak of final
judgement (he denies the authenticity of this group). Among the first
group are the traditions that God could raise up children of Abraham
from stones (Matt. 3.9), the parable that those invited to the banquet
could be replaced by others (Luke 14.15–24) and the parable of
the two sons, which ends with the words: 'Truly I tell you, the tax-
collectors and the prostitutes are going into the kingdom of God
ahead of you' (Matt. 21.31). Thus the saying in the vineyard parable
that the owner will 'destroy the tenants and give the vineyard to others'
(Mark 12.9) is not necessarily an obvious Christian interpolation, as

Vermes and Crossan maintain. If the correspondence between Israel and vineyard and tenants and leadership is intended, then the meaning of the parable is that the care of Israel will pass to others. However, if the correspondence is less precise, 'then it gave notice that those to whom the purposes and promises had been entrusted would find their possession given to others if they refused to produce fruit'.[22] In either case, Borg accepts the authenticity of the core of the parable (it has undoubtedly been embellished) and sees it as a warning against those 'to whom the purposes and promises had been entrusted'.

Conclusion

Despite the very different views of Jesus held by Vermes, Crossan and Borg, they all hold minimalist views of his use of Scripture, and for similar reasons. First, and most significant, is Markan priority, which puts a question mark against the explicit quotations and identifications in the other Gospels that are either absent or ambiguous in Mark. This virtually rules out the special material in Matthew (M), Luke (L) and the Gospel of John. Second, they all use comparative studies to show that 'son of man' and 'suffering servant' were not titles or recognized figures in first-century Judaism, and so reject those traditions where this is assumed. Third, the rejection of an apocalyptic 'son of man' figure is extrapolated to include other 'end of world' sayings, particularly as this was a characteristic of the early Church. Fourth, each is aware that down the ages, the Gospels have been subject to anti-Semitic interpretation and are therefore cautious about accepting any anti-Jewish material in the Gospels. Last, each has a view of Jesus' wisdom and insight that is regarded as incompatible with constantly citing Scripture. This is an important point to note. It might be thought that 'minimalists' are simply trying to diminish the importance of Jesus by denying that he saw himself as the fulfilment of Israel's Scriptures, but this is not the case. Rather, they believe that the Gospel writers diminished Jesus by making him the mouthpiece for their own egocentric claim that they are now the people that God will rescue from the imminent collapse of the universe.

6

Jesus and Scripture – moderate views

Introduction

In introducing this chapter, let me reiterate that I am using the term 'moderate' to describe those who believe that a 'moderate' amount of the material found in the canonical Gospels can plausibly be traced back to the historical Jesus. It is not intended to carry any moral connotations, as if 'moderate' were naturally better than 'extreme'. It is simply the recognition that some scholars believe that a case can be made for the authenticity of a moderate amount of Gospel traditions, while remaining sceptical of the Gospel of John and some of the special material in Matthew (M) and Luke (L). This is partly because they accept most of Q as a reliable early source, against the stratification theories of Kloppenborg – in turn partly because they are unwilling to accord such importance to *Gospel of Thomas*[1] – and partly because they do not restrict their explanations of Gospel differences to the literary model of Matthew and Luke rewriting Mark and Q. In particular, it is recognized that Jesus would surely have repeated his teaching on a number of occasions, which may account for some of the variations in wording that we find in the Gospels.

We will consider two types of studies in this chapter. First, there are studies that focus on a particular passage or group of passages and aim to show that a good case can be made for their authenticity. This usually involves responding to the arguments of 'minimalists' and presenting new arguments for accepting the authenticity of at least the core of the story or saying. An example of this is when a Gospel saying has similarities with the Aramaic Targum against the LXX. Thus in the blindness saying of Isaiah 6.10 ('Make the mind of this people dull, and stop their ears, and shut their eyes, so that they may not look with their eyes, and listen with their ears, and comprehend with their minds, *and turn and be healed*'), the LXX has rendered the last clause '*and turn – and I would heal them*', which is how it appears in Matthew 13.15. But in Mark 4.12 Jesus speaks of 'being forgiven', which agrees with the Targum. This does not mean that the whole of Mark 4.12 can be regarded as authentic as there are also significant differences between it and the Targum, but it suggests that Mark preserves a memory of Jesus referring to this text, even if its location – as an explanation for Jesus' parables – is likely to be of Christian origin.[2]

Second, we will look at studies that offer an overall picture of Jesus, usually by setting him within a particular trajectory of scriptural traditions. As John Meier says: 'Jesus would have been a very strange Jewish teacher in 1st-century Palestine if he had never quoted, commented on, or argued about the meaning of the Jewish Scriptures.'[3] Minimalists argue that if a particular text or tradition was being used in the early Church, then its presence in the Gospels is dubious. But moderates are inclined to reverse this: the most likely explanation for the presence of a text or tradition in the early Church is either because Jesus specifically directed his disciples towards it or said something that acted as a catalyst for its discovery.

Thus Tom Wright, in *Jesus and the Victory of God*, published in 1996, modifies the criterion of dissimilarity to include a positive element: traditions should be granted a high degree of probability if they are *somewhat different* from traditional Jewish views and later Church beliefs, but *sufficiently similar* to be plausible in a first-century Jewish context, while going some way to explaining how later Church beliefs arose. For example, minimalists reject those parables that speak of a master entrusting his property to servants until he returns (Matt. 25.14–30; Luke 19.11–27) because they look like an obvious reference to the Church's belief in the second coming. But Wright argues that a Jewish audience would most likely have 'heard' the parables as speaking about God's return to Zion, and hence the commands to be alert and prepared. This is different from the Church's view of a second coming, but it does help to explain how that belief arose. If rumours of Jesus' resurrection led to an almost apocalyptic fervour among the disciples, as minimalists maintain, it is easy to see how parables about returning masters were interpreted as prophecies of Jesus' second coming. The interpretation was incorrect but the parables themselves are genuine utterances of Jesus.[4]

Studies

Jesus the eschatological prophet

If scepticism towards Mark's framework can be traced back to William Wrede and his 1901 book, *The Messianic Secret*, discussed in the last chapter, then the view that Jesus was an eschatological prophet can be traced back to Albert Schweitzer's celebrated 1906 study that bears the English title, *The Quest of the Historical Jesus*. Schweitzer took the apocalyptic sayings at face value because:

1 they cohere with the sense of urgency that runs through the Synoptic Gospels, especially the mission charge in Matthew 10.23;
2 they are at home in contemporary Jewish works such as *Enoch*, *Psalms of Solomon* and *4 Ezra*;
3 the history of interpretation has gone to such lengths to reinterpret them in non-apocalyptic categories that they must be original.

For Schweitzer, Jesus was an apocalyptic prophet who believed that the end of the world was at hand.

Ed Sanders, in *Jesus and Judaism*, published in 1985, disagrees with Schweitzer that Jesus was an apocalyptic prophet, but agrees that eschatology – concern with the climax of God's plan for Israel – must be seen as central to Jesus' mission. Key to this is Jesus' deliberate choice of 12 disciples, which is clearly parallel to the 12 tribes of Israel. Thus the Q saying (Matt. 19.28/Luke 22.30) that the disciples would one day sit on thrones 'judging the twelve tribes of Israel' is unlikely to be an invention of the early Church, given what happened to Judas. It is more likely an authentic saying of Jesus (criterion of embarrassment), and situates him among the prophets who looked forward to the restoration and renewal of Israel (Isa. 49.5–6; 56.1–8; 66.18–24).[5]

Sanders draws attention to three symbolic acts that take place during Passion week: Jesus rides into Jerusalem on a donkey; he stages a protest against the temple; and he eats a special meal with his disciples on the evening of Passover. He does not interpret these events as indicating that Jesus saw himself as the Messiah who would die for the sins of the world, as later Christians did, but argues that they do point to a role in the restoration of Israel. The tradition that Jesus either threatened or predicted the destruction of the temple is virtually certain, which places him with those who longed for a temple 'not made with hands' (Mark 14.58), even if he did not say those precise words. In short:

Jesus saw himself as God's last messenger before the establishment of the kingdom. He looked for a new order, created by a mighty act of God. In the new order the twelve tribes would be reassembled, there would be a new temple, force of arms would not be needed, divorce would be neither necessary nor permitted, outcasts – even the wicked – would have a place, and Jesus and his disciples – the poor, meek and lowly – would have the leading role.[6]

Stephen Bryan, in *Jesus and Israel's Traditions of Judgement and Restoration*, published in 2002, focuses his study on the vineyard parables since they almost certainly go back to Jesus in some form or other. He thinks that to a first-century Jewish audience, any story about a vineyard not producing fruit would automatically suggest the allegory of Isaiah 5. Thus in the parable of the fig tree (Luke 13.6–9) a story is told about a landowner who returns to his vineyard three times in the hope of finding fruit from a particular fig tree, but finds none. He thus tells the gardener to destroy it, but the gardener responds by urging one last attempt to make it fruitful. Bryan thinks that this is a rather obvious allusion to the pathos of Isaiah 5.4 ('What more was there to do for my vineyard that I have not done in it? When I expected it to yield grapes, why did it yield wild grapes?'). The novel element in Jesus' parable is the introduction of the fig tree, an image often used for Israel's fruitfulness (blessing) or barrenness (curse). According to Bryan, Jesus does this in order to concentrate the impending judgement in one single act. In Isaiah it is described in stages – hedge removed, wall broken, trampled underfoot, laid waste, unpruned, overgrown, parched – but cutting down a fig tree is swift and decisive (cf. John the Baptist: 'Even now the axe is lying at the root of the trees'). He concludes:

> Unlike many of his contemporaries whose understanding of Israel's situation was shaped by biblical traditions which anticipated Israel's restoration and the judgement of the nation's Gentile oppressors, Jesus' expectations were heavily informed by traditions which declared that the heat of God's wrath would be vented on Israel for covenant unfaithfulness.[7]

Jesus the rejected son/stone

The parable of the vineyard is often dismissed as an attempt to explain the death of Christ and the birth of the Church, but a shorter form is also found in *Gospel of Thomas* 65. Although this lacks some of the parallels with Isaiah 5, such as the reference to the 'beloved son', we still have a story where a landowner plants a vineyard, intends to collect its fruit, sends a servant who is abused and then sends his son, who is killed. Since Jesus was in the habit of addressing God as Father (Mark 14.36; Luke 11.2), it seems likely that he was referring to himself as 'the son', though only the Synoptic accounts speak of the subsequent transfer of the vineyard to others. However, as the next saying in *Gospel of Thomas* is a quotation of Psalm 118.22, a case can be made that Jesus not only saw himself as the 'murdered son' of the parable but also as the 'rejected stone' of the psalm. The authenticity of the connection is frequently denied, but in its favour are the following:

- Isaiah 27.6 predicts a restored vineyard that will 'fill the whole world with fruit', so there is no reason to deny that Jesus could have done so.
- *Gospel of Thomas* 66 strengthens the view that Jesus quoted Psalm 118.22, and coming directly after the parable, is at least suggestive that they were originally linked.
- The link with the parable appears to be based on the similarity between the Hebrew words for 'son' (*ben*) and 'stone' (*eben*), which does not work in Greek (*huios/lithos*).
- It follows a trend found in the Aramaic Targum of Psalm 118.22 to understand the stone as a person – indeed, a very special person – 'the boy which the builders abandoned was among the sons of Jesse and he is worthy to be appointed king and ruler'.

Thus it can be freely admitted that the parable has been embellished in its retelling (the links with Isaiah 5 have been made more explicit and the rejected stone has attracted other 'stone' texts), but a case can be made that Jesus understood his fate in terms of a 'murdered son' and a 'rejected stone'.

Jesus the smitten shepherd

Taken in isolation, the quotation of Zechariah 13.7 is open to doubt. It is used to show that Jesus predicted his coming death (as the smitten shepherd) and the desertion of his disciples (as the scattered sheep), but the application is not as straightforward as minimalists suggest. First, the disciples scatter before Jesus' death and not as a result of it, and second, the context in Zechariah is God's punishment of lying prophets, hence the reference to 'striking the shepherd' appears to be negative. Thus the argument that the early Church immediately saw the relevance of this text to Christ is not persuasive. Instead Craig Evans has argued that the quotation is best seen in the light of other evidence that Jesus had Zechariah 9—14 in mind as he contemplated his Passion. First, he enters Jerusalem on a donkey – a deliberate fulfilment of Zechariah 9.9. Second, he stages an attack on the 'traders' of the temple – which might well be a fulfilment of Zechariah 14.21.[8] Third, we have the words 'blood of the covenant' at the last supper – which principally come from Exodus 24.8 but are also found in Zechariah 9.11, just after the 'entry on a donkey' verse. We might also add a fourth – that the 'scattering of the disciples' is also found in John 16.32, even if John has no interest in the 'smiting' clause. Thus a case can be made that Jesus saw his Passion in the light of Zechariah 9—14, and hence his death and the desertion of the disciples as a fulfilment of the smitten shepherd and the scattering of the sheep.[9]

Jesus the vindicated 'son of man'

The interpretation of the son of man coming in/on/with clouds provides a good example of what literary theorists call intertextuality.[10] Mark 13.26 appears to predict the coming of a supernatural being who will gather the elect from the four corners of the earth and bring an end to their suffering. The use of 'son of man', 'coming' and 'clouds' has convinced most scholars that Mark has Daniel 7.13 in mind, which in turn has influenced their interpretation of Daniel 7. It is commonly read as predicting the coming of a supernatural figure to rescue Israel from the fourth beast and usher in the kingdom of God, where 'all peoples, nations, and languages should serve him' (Dan. 7.14b). Understood in this way, it is easy to see how Mark or the tradition before him identified Jesus as that figure, and thus why minimalists are suspicious as to whether it goes back to Jesus.

However, if Daniel 7 is read on its own terms, we find that the phrase 'son of man' is closely linked with the people of Israel. Thus when Daniel asks for an interpretation of his disturbing vision, he is first told that the four beasts represent four kings that will arise from the earth, and then that it is the 'holy ones of the Most High' that will possess the kingdom (Dan. 7.17). The identification is repeated in Daniel 7.27, where 'kingship and dominion and the greatness of the kingdoms under the whole heaven shall be given to the people of the holy ones of the Most High'. The significance of this is that the son of man is not an individual who comes to rescue the suffering people of God (Dan. 7.7, 25); rather the two are inextricably linked. Thus the message of Daniel 7 is that the suffering people of God will have to endure four evil kingdoms but will ultimately inherit an eternal kingdom.

This then raises the question of whether Mark 13.26 is a misinterpretation of Daniel 7.13 or whether our understanding of Mark 13.26 needs to be revised. This task was undertaken by Morna Hooker in her landmark study, *The Son of Man in Mark*, published in 1967. After reviewing the use of the expression in Daniel 7, *1 Enoch*, *2 Esdras*, Ecclesiasticus, Wisdom of Solomon and *The Testaments of the Twelve Patriarchs*, she discusses the meaning of the sayings from Mark's beginning (Mark 2.10, 28), central section (Mark 8.31, 38; 9.9, 12, 31; 10.33f., 45) and Passion narrative (Mark 13.26; 14.21, 41, 62). Their meaning falls into three categories: the authority of the son of man on earth; the necessity of the son of man to suffer; and the future vindication and exaltation of the son of man. Her argument is that if Daniel 7 is about the suffering and vindication of the people of God, then there is no need to isolate the apocalyptic sayings of Mark 13.26 and 14.62, for the 'authority, necessity for suffering, and confidence in final vindication, which are expressed in the Marcan sayings, can all be traced to Dan. 7'.[11]

In her final chapter, Hooker asks whether this revised understanding of Mark's 'Son of Man' sayings has any bearing on the question of whether they go back to Jesus. She thinks that it does, though her language is cautious: 'this interpretation deserves consideration as *possibly* a *reasonably* reliable representation of Jesus' own use and understanding of the term'.[12] At any rate, it is more probable that Jesus identified himself with the people of Israel in their election (authority), present suffering and future vindication than that the 'Son of Man' sayings are an invention of the early Church, since the phrase hardly appears outside the Gospels.[13] It would also answer the question posed in Mark 9.12: 'How then is it written about the Son of Man, that he is to go through many sufferings and be treated with contempt?' Scholars have looked in vain for a text that speaks about the suffering of 'the Son of Man', but if the reference is to the general theme of Daniel 7, then it makes sense. Jesus will suffer and be vindicated because that is the destiny of Israel.

Jesus the interpreter of the law

Sanders' study challenged the popular view that Jesus wished to replace the legalistic religion of the Pharisees with a religion of love and forgiveness. As far as we can tell, Jesus did not break any law or encourage his followers (present or future) to do so: 'He attended synagogue, he did not eat pork, he did not work on the sabbath in any obvious way. He accepted the sacrificial system both as atoning (Matt. 5.23f.) and purifying (Mark 1.40–44).'[14] Many scholars have accepted this and indeed wish to separate themselves from the implicit prejudice that underlies past interpretations. However, others think that the blanket statement that 'Jesus kept the law' is itself in danger of becoming a new prejudice. Jesus may not have formally broken the law, but there is a significant difference between his approach to it and that of most of his contemporaries. Tom Holmén explores this in *Jesus and Jewish Covenant Thinking*, published in 2001. He introduces a concept that he calls 'covenant path searching', which he defines as the practical matters by which Jews of all persuasions demonstrated their covenant loyalty. He agrees that Jesus never formally broke the law, but argues that in a rather conspicuous way Jesus did not attempt to *demonstrate* his covenant loyalty.

For example, Holmén believes that the tradition that Jesus forbade the taking of oaths (Matt. 5.33–37) is authentic since it also occurs in James 5.12 and is contrary to later Church practice (Rom. 9.1; 2 Cor. 11.10–11, 31; Gal. 1.20). He acknowledges that forbidding something that the law permits does not amount to breaking the law, but he thinks that the absolute statement would have sounded astounding: 'The total prohibition on oaths ascribed to Jesus – very much unlike Old Testament and contemporary Jewish criticism of swearing falsely or loosely – implies criticism of the law itself. If swearing is wrong *in toto*, why is it allowed, even if discouraged, by the Scripture?'[15] Holmén thinks the same is true of Jesus' attitude to divorce. Of course, Deuteronomy 24.1–4 is not a command to divorce, but 'Jesus' prohibition on divorce cannot be taken as merely interpreting the law ... or intensifying the commandments ... Jesus' view implies that the law is inadequate and therefore to ask how to keep it is simply not the right question.'[16]

On the other hand, James Crossley denies that Jesus' words would have sounded astounding. He points out that Philo regarded abstinence of oaths as one of the ways the Essenes – probably related to the Qumran community – demonstrated their love for God. If Philo did not regard the forbidding of oaths as a criticism of the law, it is unlikely that Jesus' hearers would have regarded his teaching as astounding. And although Matthew's famous exception clause for divorce – if adultery has taken place – is clearly secondary, it may well be a correct interpretation of Mark. Mark's statement looks absolute (no divorce on any grounds), but it may assume that adultery has already broken the marriage bond; Matthew is simply making it explicit. Crossley concludes that 'in all three synoptic gospels Jesus is portrayed as a Torah observant Jew in conflict with Jews dedicated to expanding and developing the biblical laws.'[17]

James Dunn

Dunn's book, *Jesus Remembered*, published in 2003, is the first volume in a trilogy called *Christianity in the Making*, and the title is significant. What we have in the Gospels is best described as a 'performance' of the Jesus tradition as it was remembered by the early witnesses. Dunn acknowledges that the traditional solution to the Synoptic problem – Matthew and Luke used Mark and Q – is still the most likely, but thinks that far more attention needs to be given to oral tradition. Thus when he compares parallel passages the task is not so much to establish the earliest form of the tradition and discard the rest, but to discover what is 'characteristic' of the diverse performances represented in the Gospels. Sometimes the best solution is literary (that is, Matthew or Luke have deliberately changed the wording of Mark or Q), but on other occasions it is oral – they know how the material is being 'performed' in different churches. Many scholars accept this as an explanation for the different forms of the Lord's prayer in Matthew 6.9–13 and Luke 11.2–4, but Dunn extends it to non-liturgical texts: 'In short, my conviction remains that the shape and verbal variations of most of the Synoptic traditions are better explained by such an oral hypothesis than exclusively in terms of literary dependence.'[18]

A good example of this is found in his discussion of Jesus and the law, or 'hungering for what is right', as he prefers to call it. Dunn acknowledges that the Sabbath stories contain signs of 'improvement', but one should not let this detract from the obvious: Jesus was remembered as having a high regard for the Sabbath and in no sense called for its abolition; but he was also remembered for refusing to make it a test-case for obedience to God. Thus Jesus 'shows no interest in treating the Sabbath as an indicator for covenant loyalty . . . at no time, however sacred, can it be wrong to do good or save life'.[19] Similarly with the purity laws. A strict adherence to Markan priority would suggest that Matthew was unhappy with Jesus' statement that nothing is unclean in itself, and modified it accordingly. But a 'performance' paradigm might suggest that Matthew was aware that Mark was drawing on traditions from predominantly Gentile churches, and drew on traditions from more Jewish churches instead. Both streams remembered that Jesus drew a contrast between inner and outer purity, but each 'performed' them in different ways. There is no reason to think that Matthew did not like Jesus' teaching at this point; he was simply aware that it was being 'performed' differently in other churches.

According to Dunn, one of the most certain aspects of Jesus' teaching is that he referred to himself as 'Son of Man', the Aramaic phrase meaning something like 'a man like me'. It is also likely that Jesus sometimes used the phrase with Daniel's vision in mind, though Dunn thinks the dating of the *Similitudes of Enoch* is too precarious to argue that a specific title or figure was in mind. Instead he notes that Daniel 7 is part of a 'substantial tradition in Jewish thought' that the righteous will suffer for their loyalty to God, which informed Jesus' understanding of his own role.[20] This can be seen in the Passion predictions, where despite the various embellishments there is a core saying that 'the Son of Man is to be handed over into the hands of men' (Matt. 17.22; Mark 9.31; Luke 9.44). This preserves the Hebrew/Aramaic wordplay ('the man is to be handed over to the men'), and the use of the passive ('handed over') is a typical Jewish idiom. It was only when these 'Son of Man' sayings were translated into Greek (lit. 'the son of the man') that they looked like a definite title and were then drawn into traditions of returning masters (Mark 13.26) and figures at God's right hand (Mark 14.62).

Dunn thus agrees with Hooker that it is more likely that Jesus looked to Daniel 7 (and Zechariah and Psalms) than Isaiah 53 for an understanding of his suffering. He thinks that the single quotation of Isaiah 53.12 in Luke 22.37 is an obvious intrusion since it interrupts the discussion of the sword in verses 36 and 38, and that the last supper saying about 'blood poured out for many' is better understood in the light of 'covenant renewal' than 'sin offering'. Of course, the servant passages in Isaiah 40—55 are part of Israel's 'righteous suffering' tradition, and so were probably among the texts and traditions that influenced Jesus. But there is no reason to think that Jesus *specifically* saw himself as the figure described in Isaiah 53, however 'obvious' such an identification has appeared to the later Church.

Complex solutions to the Synoptic problem

It is now commonly recognized that Matthew's and Luke's use of Mark and Q does not explain all the similarities and differences between the Synoptic Gospels. This is particularly the case with the so-called 'minor agreements', where in passages common to all three (the triple tradition), Matthew and Luke agree against Mark. Thus Mark has Jesus reply 'I am' to the high priest's question about being the Messiah (Mark 14.62), but in Matthew and Luke the reply is evasive (Matt. 26.64/Luke 22.67). It is difficult to believe that Matthew and Luke both wished to remove the certainty of Mark's reply; more likely the version of Mark they were using was similarly evasive, as indeed it is in some manuscripts. Some scholars have therefore suggested 'complex' solutions to the Synoptic problem where the version of Mark used by Matthew and Luke is not the same as the version that has come down to us, and that Matthew and Luke may themselves have been subject to later editing.

Tom Wright

If Marcus Borg was a bridge between minimalist and moderate, Tom Wright is a bridge between moderate and maximalist. His lengthy description of his historical approach in *The New Testament and the People of God*, published in 1992 (as the first volume of *Christian Origins and the Question of God*), puts him firmly in the moderate category. But the results of his study in the second volume, *Jesus and the Victory of God*, published in 1996, *rarely* conclude that a saying or tradition is inauthentic. His stated aim is to produce a portrait of Jesus that can answer the following five questions:

1 How does Jesus fit into Judaism?
2 What were Jesus' aims?
3 Why did Jesus die?
4 How and why did the early Church begin?
5 Why are the Gospels what they are?

Wright does not believe that this will be accomplished by applying specific criteria to individual sayings and basing a reconstruction on what is deemed authentic, for the application of the criteria is too tied up with the author's presuppositions. For example, apocalyptic sayings are often rejected because it is assumed that they are referring to the end of the world. But if they are better considered as an 'elaborate metaphor-system for investing historical events with theological significance',[21] then the objection disappears and there is no reason to deny their authenticity.

Wright also regards the differences in wording between the Synoptic Gospels as just as likely to come from Jesus' saying things on more than one occasion as from deliberate redactional changes by Matthew or Luke. Instead of this conventional scholarly wisdom, Wright suggests that the most likely hypothesis is the one that best answers his five questions, and he finds this encapsulated in the parable of the prodigal son:

> Consider: here is a son who goes off in disgrace into a far country and then comes back, only to find the welcome challenged by another son who has stayed put . . . This is the story of Israel, in particular of exile and restoration . . . Babylon had taken the people into captivity . . . The people had returned in a geographical sense, but the great prophecies of restoration had not yet come true . . . But Israel would return, humbled and redeemed: sins would be forgiven, the covenant renewed, the Temple rebuilt, and the dead raised. What her god had done for her in the exodus – always the crucial backdrop for Jewish expectation – he would at last do again, even more gloriously. YHWH would finally become king, and would do for Israel, in covenant love, what the prophets foretold.[22]

This is the story that Jesus evokes in the parable, and the implication is that it is being fulfilled – in a way that shocks those who stayed at home – in his ministry. Wright believes that this basic storyline is both coherent and answers his five questions:

1 'Jesus fits believably into first-century Judaism, retelling its stories in new but thoroughly comprehensible ways.'
2 '[H]e believes himself, much as John the Baptist had done, to be charged with the god-given responsibility of regrouping Israel around himself . . . As a result, it is also a counter-Temple movement, and is perceived as such.'
3 'If the message is ever to be spoken or acted in Jerusalem itself, hostility will come from the Temple authorities.'
4 'If this proclamation were to end simply with the shameful death of its proclaimer, that would be that . . . But if it were vindicated after that shameful death, there would be every reason to continue to believe that the kingdom had indeed arrived, in however paradoxical a fashion.'
5 Luke retells the 'original story with an eye to this new, but theologically consistent, setting'.[23]

And over the remaining 500 pages of *Jesus and the Victory of God*, Wright attempts to show how this hypothesis can make sense of the Gospel traditions.

For example, he understands the parable of the sower in a similar way to the parable of the tenants. The sower sows the seed in the hope of obtaining a harvest, but is thwarted by the condition of the first three soils. Similarly, a man plants a vineyard and rents it out to tenants in the hope of receiving fruit, but is thwarted by the abuse and killing of his servants. In the parable of the sower the conclusion is simple: the sower at last finds good soil and a great harvest results. But in the parable of the vineyard, judgement comes upon the tenants and the harvest only comes when the vineyard is given to others. This might look like a significant difference between the two parables, but Wright explains this by referring to the blindness quotation of Isaiah 6.9–10. This is not a later piece of predestination theology but Jesus drawing on Isaiah's strange commission to preach the inevitability of judgement (Isa. 6.11–12b), followed by the hope of mercy as symbolized by 'seed' (Isa. 6.13b). Thus for Wright, the parable and its explanation make perfect sense and should be regarded as authentic. Its meaning is that:

Israel's history had reached its great climactic moment with the work of Jesus himself. The end of exile was at hand; the time of lost seed was passing away, and the time of fruit had dawned; the covenant was to be renewed; YHWH himself was returning to his people, to 'sow' his word in their midst, as he promised, and so restore their fortunes at last.[24]

As a result, Wright is able to say far more about Jesus fulfilling prophecy than most scholars because he does not focus on individual sayings but rather the broad contours of Israel's story. Thus he acknowledges that, when taken in isolation, it is difficult to be sure whether the ransom saying of Mark 10.45 or the words at the last supper in Mark 14.24 are intended to evoke Isaiah 53. But they are convincing when Jesus is seen to have told the 'second-Temple story of the suffering and exile of the people of YHWH in a new form, and proceeded to act it out, finding himself called, like Ezekiel, symbolically to undergo the fate he had announced, in symbol and word, for Jerusalem as a whole'.[25] Much of this can be deduced from the 'suffering followed by vindication' themes in Daniel, Zechariah and Psalms, but it is Isaiah 40—55 that hint that this suffering will be the 'key action in the divinely appointed plan of redemption for Israel and the world'.[26]

Conclusion

Moderates accept that Jesus' words have been embellished in transmission ('performed' as Dunn would say) but do not think this happened *ex nihilo*. We should usually expect a core saying or action to have triggered such expansions, and this is probably to be found in the earliest traditions (Mark and Q) – but not exclusively so. Matthew and Luke had access to other traditions (both oral and written), and sometimes followed them rather than Mark or Q. Thus the earliest recoverable form may be found in any of the Gospels, though with the exception of Wright, John is usually excluded from such investigations. There is a growing acceptance that Jesus understood his role in the light of certain key passages (Dan. 7; Zech. 9—14; Ps. 22; Isa. 40—55), though how he and his original hearers would have understood these texts is debated. There is also general agreement that Jesus was a law-abiding Jew who discussed and debated such matters as purity, oaths, divorce and the Sabbath in much the same way as did contemporary Jews. Later descriptions of him as 'overturn-ing' or 'annulling' the law are more the result of Christian prejudice than historical scholarship. Nevertheless, it remains a matter of debate as to whether Jesus' practice of eating with sinners, associating with the unclean and deciding what can or cannot be done on the Sabbath would have been seen as radical. Certainly criticism of the temple would be seen as subversive, just as it was in Jeremiah's day, and it was probably this that led to Jesus' arrest and death, rather than claims to be the Messiah or Son of God.

7

Jesus and Scripture – maximalist views

Introduction

A maximalist approach begins with the presupposition that the material we have in the Gospels is a reliable account of what Jesus said and did. This usually coincides with a particular confessional stance that the Scriptures are the word of God and can therefore be trusted, but it can also be defended on other grounds. For example, as we have seen in the previous two chapters, the application of the so-called criteria of authenticity – embarrassment, dissimilarity, multiple attestation – has not resulted in a consensus but a huge variety of reconstructions, from wandering Cynic philosopher (Crossan) to eschatological prophet (Sanders) to Jewish Messiah (Wright). A maximalist will argue that this shows that there is nothing 'objective' about these criteria; they simply allow scholars to declare inauthentic those traditions that do not cohere with their particular view of Jesus. This would of course be denied by the scholars themselves, but it is precisely the accusation they make against one another.

A second issue for maximalists is the rigid application of source criticism for determining authentic tradition. One of the major reasons for undertaking the quest for the historical Jesus is that the Gospels differ among themselves, and one of the most important ways of explaining this has been the hypothesis that Matthew and Luke used Mark as one of their sources. This has resulted in a negative verdict on the material unique to Matthew and Luke and on almost all of John, but as we have seen, there are at least two other explanations for the differences. First, Jesus would no doubt have repeated his teaching on a number of occasions, and might well have varied the wording. Second, even when we are dealing with the same incident, it is likely that Jesus said far more than the few words that each Gospel records. Thus rather than explain the differences as deliberate changes by Matthew or Luke to bolster their own theologies, it may be that they have recorded a different selection of what was said.

For example, most scholars explain the story of Jesus reading from the scroll of Isaiah and claiming its fulfilment (Luke 4.21) as Luke's artful expansion of the rejection story in Mark 6.2–4. The similarities between the stories – Jesus returns to Nazareth, preaches in the synagogue, causes offence because the crowd know his family and responds by quoting a proverb about prophets being rejected by their own – are said to confirm that we are dealing with the same incident. However, maximalists argue that the differences outweigh the similarities and show that we are *not* dealing with the same incident. Thus Luke's account differs from Mark 6.2–4 in the following ways:

1 The story comes at the beginning of Jesus' ministry.
2 The crowd refer to Jesus as Joseph's son rather than Mary's son.
3 Jesus quotes the proverb 'Doctor, heal yourself'.
4 Jesus cites the examples of Elisha and Elijah having a mission to non-Israelites.
5 The incident ends with Jesus being driven out of town.

So while the similarities might suggest that we have two divergent accounts of the same event, the differences suggest that we are dealing with two quite separate incidents. And since many scholars accept that Jesus referred to Isaiah 61 in his reply to John the Baptist (and perhaps also in the beatitudes), there is no intrinsic reason why he could not have read from this passage in a synagogue service.

A third issue concerns when a passage appears to reflect the high Christology of the early Church. For example, Jesus might have thought of himself as the Messiah, the son of David, but the dialogue concerning the meaning of Psalm 110.1 ('The Lord said to my Lord, "Sit at my right hand, until I put your enemies under your feet"' – Matt. 22.44/Mark 12.36) seems to imply that Jesus thought of himself as divine. Furthermore, the argument appears to depend on the LXX, which uses *kyrios* ('lord') for both God (YHWH) and the person addressed as 'my lord' (*adonai*). However, this may be a case of later Christians reading too much into the text and then critical scholars declaring it inauthentic. The point of the debate is the paradox that the Messiah will be superior to David (he calls him 'lord'), while also being a descendant ('his son'). There is no need to suggest that Jesus understood David to be calling his son 'God' and then identifying with such a figure. All that is required is the recognition that a descendant of David (the Messiah) will be greater than David, though one should not underestimate the size of that claim. Had this dialogue been invented by the early Church, one might have expected Jesus' identification with the figure addressed in the psalm to be more explicit.

Charles Kimball

Kimball confines himself to a study of Luke's Gospel, and begins by challenging each of the so-called criteria of authenticity. He accepts that the Gospel writers both 'selected' and 'reshaped' the traditions that came down to them, but denies that there is any evidence that they invented sayings *de novo*. He cites Howard Marshall's conclusions that Luke is a reliable historian,[1] and concludes that we can be 'confident that the Jesus tradition as it is preserved in the canonical Gospels is historically reliable, and consequently also that Jesus was an expositor of the OT as the Gospels depict him'.[2] He then has a chapter on the 'Exegetical Milieu of Luke's Gospel' in which he discusses the seven exegetical rules (*middoth*) attributed to rabbi Hillel and various forms of midrash ('interpretation', from the verb 'to search') found in later rabbinic writings. One such form is known as the *proem* ('opening'), and follows this pattern:

1 The (Pentateuchal) text for the day is cited.
2 A second text, the *proem* is introduced, which 'opens' the initial text for interpretation.
3 An exposition follows, which might include supplementary quotations, parables and other commentary with verbal links to the quoted texts.
4 A final text is quoted, usually repeating or alluding to the text for the day, and sometimes adding a concluding application.

The *yelammedenu rabbenu* ('let our master teach us') form is similar except that the *proem* text takes the form of a question. It is Kimball's contention that much of Jesus' use of Scripture in Luke's Gospel reflects these exegetical patterns, and he uses this as an argument for their authenticity. He begins with the temptation narrative (Luke 4.1–13), noting that the three specific temptations – turning stones to bread, gaining authority over the world by worshipping the devil, and jumping from the temple to instigate a miracle – are hardly characteristic of the temptations faced by the early Church. Indeed, there is a rabbinic parallel (*Deuteronomy Rabbah* 11.5) where the Angel of Death quotes from the psalms (118.17; 19.2) and Moses responds by quoting from Deuteronomy (32.1, 3, 4). The written form of this tradition is centuries later than Jesus, but it was hardly borrowed from the Gospels; it could well represent an oral tradition known in Jesus' day. Kimball concludes that the best explanation for the presence of the three temptations is not the creative imagination of the early Church but an actual attempt to get Jesus to betray his messianic mission. In particular, the context of the 40 days in the wilderness and the three quotations from Deuteronomy show that Jesus saw his role in contrast to the failures of Israel: 'Jesus as the Son of God remains faithful to God and his messianic mission where Israel, God's OT son, failed to obey him'.[3] They also show that Scripture forms the basis for Jesus' understanding of his messianic identity.

Kimball then turns to the Nazareth sermon, where Jesus explicitly reads from Isaiah 61 and claims that it is being fulfilled in him. As well as the question of its relationship to Mark 6.2–4 there is also a difficulty with the text from which Jesus is said to have read: it includes the phrase 'recovery of sight to the blind', which is only found in the LXX, along with a phrase from Isaiah 58.6 ('let the oppressed go free'), which is best explained by the occurrence of the Greek word *aphesis* ('go free') in both texts. Some have tried to counter this by arguing that the link might have come about by the presence of the word 'acceptable' in the verse before (Isa. 58.5) or 'poor' in the verse after (Isa. 58.7), but Kimball accepts that it is *aphesis* that offers the best explanation. However, he does not regard this as evidence that Luke *invented* the reading, but regards it – and what follows – as a summary of the sermon that Jesus would have preached after the reading.

In his analysis he makes three points. First, Jesus interprets Scripture prophetically. Isaiah 61.1 was understood at Qumran as predicting a future figure, and Jesus explicitly claims to be that figure. Further, the introduction of the phrase from Isaiah 58.6 shows that Jesus not only thought of himself as the 'herald' of liberation but also as the 'agent' through whom it would come. Second, Jesus interprets

Scripture typologically. The stories of Elijah and Elisha were not predictions awaiting fulfilment but *narratives* of Israel's history. However, Jesus is citing them not just as general examples of people called to minister outside of Israel. Jesus sees these two great prophets as a 'pattern' for his own ministry, which is precisely what causes offence: 'When Jesus commented on Isa. 61.1–2, his audience expected blessings for them and judgment for their enemies. Consequently, they could not accept his extension of the blessings of the messiah to all people.'[4] Third, the pattern of combining texts through a catchword ('go free'), illustrating its meaning through scriptural examples and ending with other texts has some similarities with the rabbinic *proem* form, though he acknowledges that the opening text is not from the law and the final texts do not allude back to the opening text.

A much better example of rabbinic-style exegesis is found in the parable of the Good Samaritan. Here the discussion begins by citing the texts to love God and neighbour from the law (Deut. 6.5; Lev. 19.18), which share the word *agapeseis* ('you shall love'). A further text is introduced (Lev. 18.5) about 'doing the law', followed by a parable in which Jesus clarifies the meaning of 'neighbour' and 'doing', ending with a reference back to Leviticus 18.5 ('Go and *do* likewise'). The parable is regarded as authentic by almost all scholars, but the link with the lawyer's questions has been doubted. Kimball regards the questions ('what must I do to inherit eternal life?'; 'who is my neighbour?') as indicative of a *yelammedenu rabbenu* form and thus an argument for the authenticity of the connection.

Another example occurs in the parable of the vineyard, and like the Nazareth sermon, Jesus begins with a reference to Isaiah. He then tells a parable that clarifies its key terms, and ends with a number of 'stone' texts (Ps. 118.22; Isa. 8.14–15; Dan. 2.34–35) that link to the parable by the word play 'son'/'stone'. Kimball also notes that in the original parable in Isaiah 5, 'stones' have to be cleared before the vines are planted. Thus the final texts can be seen to look back to the initial text, as well as the parable. This seems rather speculative as this detail of Isaiah 5 is not mentioned by Luke (or the other Gospels), and looks more like Kimball attempting to force the *proem* pattern on the material. Nevertheless, the general observation that Jesus made use of traditional patterns of Jewish exegesis is well made, though it is doubtful that this can be used as an argument for authenticity. The variations even in the three examples discussed above show that it would be hazardous to argue that such and such a feature must be authentic because the *proem* form demands it. If these passages are authentic, they show that Jesus was aware of such patterns but used them with considerable freedom, and was certainly not tied to any particular form of them. In summary, Kimball says:

> In teaching his various Jewish audiences and in debating with the establishment theologians, he employed many of the exegetical methods commonly used by the religious teachers of Judaism. Yet he frequently offered interpretations of Scripture that were radically different from the other teachers of his day because of his superior understanding of Scripture and because of his application of the Old Testament to himself.[5]

Hillel's seven exegetical rules

It is unclear whether these rules were intended to be prescriptive (This is how you do it) or descriptive (This is how it has been done). They are usually known by their Hebrew names but in English they may be summarized as follows:

1 An inference drawn from a minor premise to a major premise and vice versa (*Qal wahomer*).
2 An inference drawn from the same word or phrase in another text (*Gezerah shawah*).
3 A general principle established on the basis of a teaching contained in one verse (*Binyan ab mikatub ehad*).
4 A general principle established on the basis of a teaching contained in two verses (*Binyan ab mishene ketubim*).
5 An inference drawn from a general principle in the text to a specific example and vice versa (*Kelal uperat uperat ukelal*).
6 An inference drawn from an analogous passage elsewhere (*Kayose bo mimaqom aher*).
7 An interpretation of a word or passage from its context (*Dabar halamed meinyano*).[6]

Richard France

France's study, *Jesus and the Old Testament*, published in 1971, focuses on Jesus' application of Scripture to himself and does not therefore discuss issues of divorce, oaths and purity laws. He does comment on Jesus' attitude to the Sabbath, however, since he is interested in Jesus' reference to 'what David did' as warrant for what he and his disciples are doing. He dismisses the idea that Jesus is using the story as a precedent for breaking the law since this would be 'inconsistent with Jesus' scrupulous attitude to the law as witnessed elsewhere in the Gospels'.[7] Instead, he considers it to be an example of typology, whereby events and people in the Old Testament are seen as 'types' or 'patterns' of God's action that are now being repeated. Other examples are the references to Jonah, Solomon, Elijah and Elisha. Thus the point of the story is that one greater than David is present, and if David had the authority to reinterpret the law, then so does Jesus. He then notes that in Matthew's version of the story, Jesus adds the words: 'Or have you not read in the law that on the sabbath the priests in the temple break the sabbath and yet are guiltless? I tell you, something greater than the temple is here' (Matt. 12.5–6). France uses this to confirm that the argument takes the form of 'one greater than David is here', though he does not explain how Matthew's 'break the Sabbath' is adequately expressed as 'reinterpreting' the Sabbath.

Having dealt with typology, France turns to Jesus' use of Old Testament prediction, focusing particularly on Daniel 7.13–14, Isaiah 53 and Zechariah 9—14. In his view the theme of Mark 13.5–23 is clearly the events leading up to the fall of Jerusalem, which coheres perfectly with the lesson of the fig tree in Mark 13.28–29 ('when you see these things taking place, you know that he is near') and Mark 13.30 ('Truly I tell you, this generation will not pass away until all these things have taken place'). It is thus unlikely that the intervening section, Mark 13.24–27, refers to a period after this, despite the flamboyant language of sun darkening, moon failing, stars falling and the Son of Man coming in clouds. Thus like Hooker he thinks that Jesus used Daniel 7.13 in much the same sense as the original – vindication and exaltation expressed in apocalyptic language.

However, France does not think that the early Church was mistaken in its view of a second coming, for he takes the final verse of the discourse ('But about that day or hour no one knows, neither the angels in heaven, nor the Son, but only the Father' – Mark 13.32) to be a veiled reference to the Old Testament's 'day of the Lord' tradition. Most commentators have taken this verse to refer to the apocalyptic drama of Mark 13.26–27, but France argues that the change from 'those days' (Mark 13.17, 20, 24) to 'that day' (Mark 13.32) is deliberate. Having prophesied the fall of Jerusalem within a generation, Jesus then turns to the final day and acknowledges that even he does not know its timing.[8] Thus France has neatly solved the difficulty raised by Schweitzer (that Jesus prophesied the imminent end of the world and was wrong): Jesus did not expect the end of the world within a generation but rather the fall of Jerusalem, and this was proved correct. As for the end of the world ('that day'), this is left as an indefinite period in the future.[9]

Concerning Jesus' identification with the servant of Isaiah 53, France begins with the explicit quotation in Luke 22.37 ('And he was counted among the lawless'). He denies the view that Jesus is simply referring to a miscarriage of justice whereby he will die among criminals, for that is hardly compatible with the solemn way that its fulfilment is described ('indeed what is written about me is being fulfilled'). This shows that it is not just a casual reference: Jesus is thinking about the fate of the figure described in the quotation, namely the suffering servant of Isaiah 53. He then looks at the ransom saying in Mark 10.45 ('For the Son of Man came not to be served but to serve, and to give his life a ransom for many') and the words at the last supper in Mark 14.24 ('This is my blood of the covenant, which is poured out for many'). He acknowledges Hooker's point that Mark's Greek differs significantly from the LXX, but he does not regard this as fatal. The thought of the passages (giving up/pouring out his life for many) is so similar to the theme of Isaiah 53 that it cannot be accidental. Indeed, the criticism that it is only the ordinary word 'many' that links the passages is itself an argument for authenticity. If the early Church wanted to show that Jesus saw himself as the suffering servant of Isaiah 53, they would hardly have made the vague word 'many' the only explicit link. The presence of this word and the theme of suffering on behalf of others confirms that Jesus had Isaiah 53 in mind – it is a tribute to the faithfulness of those who passed on the tradition that it was not turned into something more explicit.

Next he looks at the Passion predictions where Jesus indicates not only the probability of his death but its *necessity*. Hooker argued that Jesus derived the idea of his suffering from the persecution of the saints in Daniel 7, but that passage says nothing about the *necessity* of suffering or that the suffering is *on behalf* of others. On the other hand: 'Isaiah 53, poetic as it is, gives a systematic exposition of the nature, necessity and purpose of the suffering of the Messiah, which is true of no other passage in the Old Testament.'[10] France concludes by saying that:

> Jesus saw his mission as that of the Servant of Yahweh, that he predicted that in fulfilment of that role he must suffer and die, and that he regarded his suffering and death as, like that of the Servant, vicarious and redemptive.[11]

In Zechariah 9—14 a number of figures are described: a humble king riding on an ass (9.9–10); an ideal shepherd (11.4–17); someone who has been pierced, which will cause people to mourn (12.10—13.1); and a smitten shepherd (13.7). Reading these chapters, one would not necessarily get the impression that these are one and the same person, but France thinks this was undoubtedly Jesus' view. This is shown by the explicit quotation of the smitten shepherd text in Mark 14.27 and the reference to all the tribes of the earth mourning in Matthew 24.30, which is an allusion to Zechariah 12.10. Add to this the entry into Jerusalem on a donkey as a fulfilment of Zechariah 9.9–10, and the protest against the traders as a fulfilment of Zechariah 14.21, and the conclusion is obvious: Jesus saw himself fulfilling the various roles described in Zechariah 9—14.[12] The significance of this for France is that instead of quoting from texts that predict the messiah's victory over his enemies, Jesus cites texts from Zechariah that speak of a 'lowly king, rejected and killed by the people to whom he comes, whose martyrdom is the cause of their repentance and salvation'.[13]

In his final chapter, France considers the 'originality' and 'influence' of Jesus. At one level there are similarities between Jesus and his fellow interpreters. He shares the same reverence for the texts, abides by their teaching and uses similar methods of exegesis. However, his application of 'suffering' texts to his earthly ministry, and 'victory' texts to the resurrection and beyond, is without parallel: 'The reason for this was not just that he was a creative thinker with new ideas, but that he was the one "of whom Moses in the law and also the prophets wrote", and that he himself knew this'.[14] Luke's description of Jesus opening the minds of the disciples so that they could understand how the Scriptures speak about him is the best explanation for the creative use of Scripture by the early Church.[15] France concludes:

> While second to none in his reverence for the Scriptures, his diligent study of them and his acceptance of their teaching, and while employing an exegesis which differed from that of his contemporaries generally only in a closer adherence to the original sense where misunderstanding or misuse was the rule, he yet applied the Old Testament in a way which was quite unparalleled. The essence of his new application was that he saw the fulfilment of the predictions and foreshadowings of the Old Testament in himself and his work.[16]

Conclusion

Kimball and France both acknowledge that Jesus' use of Scripture has much in common with his fellow Jewish interpreters, but what sets him apart is the way that he applies particular texts to his own life and ministry. Kimball puts this down to his 'superior understanding of Scripture', and France suggests that Jesus had a 'closer adherence to the original sense' of the texts than his contemporaries, where 'misunderstanding or misuse was the rule'. Both comments illustrate the confessional nature of their positions because they only make sense if Jesus' claims are regarded as true. The fact that his fellow Jewish interpreters were not looking for a 'suffering servant', 'smitten shepherd' or 'pierced one' could suggest that Jesus' interpretations are *not* those that naturally emerge from the language and grammar of the texts. Thus the question of whether Jesus' interpretations are closer to the original meaning depends on whether one believes that the prophets were inspired by God to speak about Jesus, even though they appear to be speaking about their own situation or at least the immediate future.

Indeed, many of the texts cited by Jesus (see Appendix 1) are not prophecies in the traditional sense, something both Kimball and France make use of 'typology' to explain. This goes further than saying that Jesus saw David, Solomon, Elijah and Jonah as examples for his own ministry; it is more that certain aspects of their lives 'prefigured' certain aspects of his, though not in the form of future-tense prophecy. Again, it would be difficult to argue that this represents a 'closer adherence to the original sense' unless one believes, with

Luke, that *everything* written in the law, prophets and psalms refers to Jesus (Luke 24.44). Scholars from our first two categories (except Wright?) find this impossible to accept, but Kimball and France can at least claim that their interpretations are the ones the Gospels themselves commend.

Conclusion

In the last three chapters we have seen how scholars use a variety of arguments and evidence to determine how Jesus used Scripture. However, it has also become clear that alongside arguments and evidence there is a third element, which I shall call conviction. Conviction is not quite the same thing as faith since its focus is not necessarily religious. For example, a key issue in our study has been whether it is possible to devise criteria to distinguish between authentic and inauthentic tradition. This is not necessarily a 'faith' question since it could apply to the study of any ancient document. Some scholars think it is possible to devise such criteria, even if the results turn out to be minimal. Others think that such criteria simply reflect the presuppositions of the individual scholar; there is nothing 'neutral' or 'objective' about them.

However, some convictions are religious. Scholars such as Crossan and Vermes are convinced that the early Church substantially changed the message of Jesus – they see their task as restoring his original teaching. There is an almost missionary zeal about their books, urging the Church to recognize that its traditional doctrines are based on a distortion of Jesus' teaching. This is clearly an attractive view for those who feel alienated by institutional religion, and it would be naive to think that it does not play a role in one's assessment of the historical data. At the heart of this view is the conviction that Jesus spoke on his own authority and did not seek to bolster his teaching by references to Scripture. This is what set him apart from his fellow Jews. Thus while Vermes says that Scripture 'played a fundamental part in the religious and literary creativity of the Jews in the intertestamental era when the Apocrypha, Pseudepigrapha, the Dead Sea Scrolls and the earliest rabbinic writings were produced',[1] Jesus was different. His vision derived from his mystical/spiritual union with God, and he spoke 'as one having authority, and not as the scribes' (Mark 1.22). Unfortunately, as is often the way with prophets and charismatics, those who came after him misunderstood his message: by the time we get to the Gospels, Jesus is being portrayed as an interpreter and exegete of Scripture.

On the other hand, moderates and maximalists believe that this reconstruction turns Jesus into an anomaly, cut off from his Jewish background and divorced from the early Church. Something has to account for the emergence of a set of documents in the second half of the first century that contain over 300 quotations from Scripture. The documents themselves identify this something as Jesus' own use of Scripture, so why should we look for anything else? Maximalists take this to mean that all of the quotations found in the Gospels should be regarded as the actual words of Jesus, even when the wording differs from one Gospel to another. After all, if texts such as Isaiah 6.9, Psalm 110.1 and Daniel 7.13 were important to Jesus, he would no doubt have quoted them on a number of occasions. Moderates, however, are unconvinced by this argument, believing that the differences found in the Gospels demonstrate that some form of theological development has taken place. For them, the explanation that best fits the data is that Jesus was the *catalyst* for the extensive use of Scripture found in the Gospels and the rest of the New Testament. Put simply, Jesus interpreted Scripture in the light of what God was about to do; the early Church interpreted Jesus (and Scripture) in the light of what God had done.

Thus another conviction that affects how one evaluates the evidence concerns the validity or otherwise of theological development. This takes two forms. The first is general and can be put like this: do texts have fixed meanings or can meaning change over time? For example, if the psalmist was thinking of King David when he uttered 'The LORD says to my lord, "Sit at my right hand until I make your enemies your footstool"' (Ps. 110.1), can it ever be valid to apply these words to someone else? Interestingly, maximalists and minimalists have something in common here in that they both regard such a change as invalid. The difference is that minimalists assign the change to the early Church, while maximalists deny that any (significant) change has taken place. They argue that the exalted language of Psalm 110 shows that the psalmist was *not* thinking (exclusively) about King David, but looked forward to a greater king where such prophecies would apply. Moderates are more inclined to acknowledge that a change of meaning has taken place, but point out that this was perfectly acceptable in Jesus' first-century context. Indeed, first-century interpreters would have been perplexed by our modern fixation with discovering the 'original meaning' of a text. For them, the whole point of Scripture is that it speaks to the present, so that the task of interpretation is not to recover something called 'original meaning' but to show how a text applies/speaks to the present. Interestingly, modern literary theory is also more interested in the ongoing life of a text than focusing on the original intentions of its author.[2]

The second aspect of theological development is more specific: can it ever be valid to put words into someone's mouth that were not actually spoken? One's first response is probably an emphatic 'No', especially as Jesus' message is concerned with truth and integrity. Thus it is one thing for Matthew 8.17 to assert that Jesus' healing miracles are a fulfilment of Isaiah 53; that is Matthew's theological assessment and one can choose to agree or disagree with it. However, it is quite another for Luke 22.37 to state that just before the crucifixion, Jesus explicitly quoted from Isaiah 53, if in fact he did not do so. Once again, minimalists respond by assigning Luke 22.37 to the early Church, while maximalists insist that Jesus must have said it. But is there a third option that sees Matthew 8.17 and Luke 22.37 as two different strategies for making the same theological point? As we saw in Chapter 1, it is possible that Mark thought that Jesus identified with Isaiah's servant, but from this distance we cannot be sure; the evidence is ambiguous. But perhaps Matthew and Luke *were* sure and decided to make it more explicit for the reader, the one by adding a comment, the other by adding an explicit quotation. The effect on the reader is much the same, namely to confirm that Jesus identified with Isaiah's servant. And if that was in fact the case, then the Gospels have led the reader to an accurate understanding of Jesus, though in Luke's case, not to his actual words. Some will still find it difficult to accept the validity of such an approach, especially as Luke claims in his introduction (1.1–4) to have carefully researched his topic, but it should be noted that many scholars think that John's Gospel consists almost entirely of this type of writing (sometimes known as 'narrative theology').[3]

This has been a historical study to determine how Jesus used Scripture, first by presenting the evidence from the Gospels and second by considering three major approaches (minimalist, moderate, maximalist) to its assessment. Writing history is not a neutral investigation of 'facts' but a working hypothesis based on evidence, arguments and convictions. Though I have tried to be fair to all of the scholars I have discussed, it will come as no surprise to readers that I identify most with the 'moderates'. I find it difficult to believe that Scripture was vitally important to Jews and vitally important to Christians but not important to Jesus. On the other hand, I find that the differences between the Gospels make it difficult to accept a maximalist position that Jesus said everything the Gospels say he did. But the purpose of this book is not to propagate my conclusions; it is to encourage readers to work out their own. And to help with that, I have included a select bibliography through which to follow up on the scholars, texts and ideas that may have been found of most interest. Jesus' use of Scripture is a fascinating topic and still the subject of much scholarly research.

Appendix 1
Index of Jesus' quotations in the Gospels

* Texts marked with an asterisk are quoted elsewhere in the New Testament

Genesis
1.27   Matt. 19.4; Mark 10.6
2.24*   Matt. 19.5; Mark 10.7
5.2   Matt. 19.5; Mark 10.6

Exodus
3.6*   Matt. 22.32; Mark 12.26;
        Luke 20.37
12.46   John 19.36
20.12–16 Matt. 19.18–19;
        Mark 10.19; Luke 18.20
20.12* Matt. 15.4; Mark 7.10
20.13* Matt. 5.21
20.14* Matt. 5.27
21.17   Matt. 15.4; Mark 7.10
21.24   Matt. 5.38

Leviticus
19.12   Matt. 5.33
19.18* Matt. 5.43; 19.19; 22.39;
        Mark 12.31, 33;
        Luke 10.27
24.20   Matt. 5.38

Numbers
30.2   Matt. 5.33

Deuteronomy
5.16*   Matt. 15.4; Mark 7.10
5.17*   Matt. 5.21
5.18   Matt. 5.27
6.4–5   Mark 12.29–30

6.5   Matt. 22.37; Mark 12.30,
        33; Luke 10.27
6.13   Matt. 4.10; Luke 4.8
6.16   Matt. 4.7; Luke 4.12
8.3   Matt. 4.4; Luke 4.4
19.15* Matt. 18.16
19.21   Matt. 5.38
24.1–3 Matt. 5.31; 19.7; Mark 10.4

Psalms
8.2   Matt. 21.16
22.1   Matt. 27.46; Mark 15.34
31.5   Luke 23.46
35.19   John 15.25
41.9   John 13.18
69.4   John 15.25
69.9*   John 2.17
78.2   Matt. 13.35
78.24   John 6.31
82.6   John 10.34
91.11–12 Matt. 4.6; Luke 4.10–11
110.1* Matt. 22.44; 26.64;
        Mark 12.36; 14.62;
        Luke 20.42–43
118.22* Matt. 21.42; Mark 12.10;
        Luke 20.17
118.23 Matt. 21.42; Mark 12.11
118.26 Matt. 23.39; Luke 13.35

Isaiah
6.9–10* Matt. 13.14–15;
        Mark 4.12; Luke 8.10

Appendix 2
Jewish legal texts

The Mishnah is generally thought to have been completed around 200 CE and contains the pronouncements of various rabbis organized into six sections (seeds, set-feasts, women, damages, holy things, clean things), each of which is sub-divided into tractates, such as Sabbath, divorce, vows, oaths and tithes. A parallel work is the Tosefta, though its relation to the Mishnah is much debated. The difficult question is discerning which of the pronouncements would have been operative in Jesus' day, especially as the destruction of Jerusalem in 70 CE caused a massive reorganization of Jewish belief and practice. This is where the Dead Sea Scrolls have the advantage, though this must be balanced by the sectarian nature of the community that produced them. The most important legal texts among the Dead Sea Scrolls are the *Community Rule* (1QS), the *Damascus Document* (CD) and the *Temple Scroll* (11QT). The extracts below give something of the flavour of legal debate in the first century, though it is often difficult to be more definite. They are taken from the translations by Danby (Mishnah) and Vermes (Dead Sea Scrolls).*

Sabbath

No man shall work on the sixth day from the moment when the sun's orb is distant by its own fullness from the gate (wherein it sinks) . . . No man shall speak any vain or idle word on the Sabbath day. He shall make no loan to his companion. He shall make no decision in matters of money and gain. He shall say nothing about work or labour to be done on the morrow. No man shall walk in the field to do business on the Sabbath. He shall not walk more than one thousand cubits beyond his town. No man shall eat on the Sabbath day except that which is already prepared . . . No man shall walk more than two thousand cubits after a beast to pasture it outside his town . . . No man shall take anything out of the house or bring anything in . . . No man shall assist a beast to give birth on the Sabbath day. And if it should fall into a cistern or pit,

---

* Herbert Danby, *The Mishnah* (Oxford: Oxford University Press, 1933); Geza Vermes, *The Complete Dead Sea Scrolls in English* (London: Allen Lane, 1997).

he shall not lift it out on the Sabbath. No man shall spend the Sabbath in a place near to Gentiles on the Sabbath. No man shall profane the Sabbath for the sake of riches or gain on the Sabbath day. But should any man fall into water or (fire), let him not be pulled out with the aid of a ladder or rope or (some such) utensil . . . But no man who strays so as to profane the Sabbath and the feasts shall be put to death; it shall fall to men to keep him in custody . . . The Rule for the assembly of the towns of Israel shall be according to these precepts that they may distinguish between unclean and clean, and discriminate between the holy and the profane. (CD 10.15—12.19)

A great general rule have they laid down concerning the Sabbath: whosoever, forgetful of the principle of the Sabbath, committed many acts of work on many Sabbaths, is liable only to one Sin-offering . . . The main classes of work are forty save one: sowing, ploughing, reaping, binding sheaves, threshing, winnowing, cleansing crops, grinding, sifting, kneading, baking, shearing wool, washing or beating or dyeing it, spinning, weaving, making two loops, weaving two threads, separating two threads, tying [a knot], loosening [a knot], sewing two stitches, tearing in order to sew two stitches, hunting a gazelle, slaughtering or flaying or salting it or curing its skin, scraping it or cutting it up, writing two letters, erasing in order to write two letters, building, pulling down, putting out a fire, lighting a fire, striking with a hammer and taking out aught from one domain into another. (*m. Shabbat* 7:1–2)

If his teeth pain him he may not suck vinegar through them but he may take vinegar after his usual fashion, and if he is healed he is healed . . . Kings' children may anoint their wounds with rose-oil since it is their custom so to do on ordinary days. (*m. Shabbat* 14:4)

If a man has a pain in his throat they may drop medicine into his mouth on the Sabbath, since there is doubt whether life is in danger, and whenever there is doubt whether life is in danger this overrides the Sabbath. (*m. Yoma* 8:6)

Divorce

The 'builders of the wall' (Ezek. xiii, 10) who have followed after 'Precept' – 'Precept' . . . shall be caught in fornication twice by taking a second wife while the first is alive, whereas the principle of creation is, *Male and female created He them* (Gen. i, 27). Also, those who entered the Ark went in two by two. And concerning the prince it is written, *He shall not multiply wives to himself* (Deut. xvii, 17); but David had not read the sealed book of the Law which was in the ark (of the Covenant) . . . (CD 4.20–5.3)

He shall not marry as wife any daughter of the nations, but shall take a wife for himself from his father's house, from his father's family. He shall not take another wife in addition to her, for she alone shall be with him all the time of her life. But if she dies, he may marry another from his father's house, from his family. (11QT 57.17–19)

If a man divorced his wife and said to her, 'Thou art free to marry any man excepting such-a-one', R. Eliezer permits it, but the Sages forbid it. (*m. Gittin* 9:1)

The School of Shammai say: A man may not divorce his wife unless he has found unchastity in her, for it is written, *Because he hath found in her* indecency *in anything*. And the School of Hillel say: [He may divorce her] even if she spoiled a dish for him, for it is written, *Because he hath found in her indecency in* anything. R. Akiba says: Even if he found another fairer than she, for it is written, *And it shall be if she find no favour in his eyes* ... (*m. Gittin* 9:10)

Oaths and vows

Whoever approaches the Council of the Community shall enter the Covenant of God in the presence of all who have freely pledged themselves. He shall undertake by a binding oath to return with all his heart and soul to every commandment of the Law of Moses in accordance with all that has been revealed of it to the sons of Zadok ... (1QS 5.8)

(he shall not) swear by (the Name), nor by *Aleph* and *Lamed* (Elohim), nor by *Aleph* and *Daleth* (Adonai), but a binding oath by the curses of the Covenant. He shall not mention the Law of Moses for ... were he to swear and then break (his oath) he would profane the name. (CD 15.1–2)

If a man saw another eating [his] figs and said, 'May they be Korban to you!' and they were found to be his father and brothers and others with them, the School of Shammai say: For them the vow is not binding, but for the others with them it is binding. And the School of Hillel say: The vow is binding for neither of them. (*m. Nedarim* 3:2)

It once happened that a man at Beth Horon, whose father was forbidden by vow to have any benefit from him, was giving his son in marriage, and he said to his fellow, 'The courtyard and the banquet are given to thee as a gift, but they are thine only that my father may come and eat with us at the banquet'. His fellow said, 'If they are mine, they are dedicated to Heaven'. The other answered, 'I did not give thee what is mine that thou shouldest dedicate it to Heaven'. His fellow said, 'Thou didst give me what is thine only that thou and thy father might eat and drink and be reconciled one with the other, and that the sin should rest on his head!' When the case came before the Sages, they said: Any gift which, if a man would dedicate it, is not accounted dedicated, is not a [valid] gift. (*m. Nedarim* 5:6)

Purity

A woman with a seven-day issue of blood shall not touch a man with a flux, nor any vessel touched by a man who has a flux [gonorrhoea?], nor anything he has lain on or sat on ... Neither shall she touch any woman with a long-term issue of blood ... (*Tohorot A*, 4Q274 1.4–7)

A High Priest or a Nazirite may not contract uncleanness because of their [dead] kindred, but they may contract uncleanness because of a neglected corpse. (*m. Nazir* 7:1)

Thus if a man's hands were clean and the outer part of the cup was unclean, and he held it by its holding-place, he need not scruple lest his hands be made unclean by the outer part of the cup. If a man was drinking from a cup whose outer part was unclean, he need not scruple lest the liquid in his mouth be made unclean ... (*m. Kelim* 25:8)

The water may be poured over the hands out of any vessel ... It may not be poured over the hands out of the sides of [broken] vessels or out of the flanks of a ladling-jar or out of the plug of a jar, nor may a man pour it over his fellow's hands out of his cupped hands ... (*m. Yadaim* 1:2)

The Sadducees say, We cry out against you, O ye Pharisees, for ye declare clean an unbroken stream of liquid. The Pharisees say, We cry out against you, O ye Sadducees, for ye declare clean a channel of water that flows from a burial ground. (*m. Yadaim* 4:7)

Notes

Introduction

1 Some scholars object to the term Septuagint as it could suggest a single volume of authorized writings rather than a collection that has had a complex textual history. It is an important point, but the term is still the most convenient way of referring to the Greek rather than Hebrew Scriptures.

2 An additional complexity is that the LXX was itself subject to revision, as can be seen by the discovery of the Minor Prophets scroll at Nahal Hever, which differs significantly from the LXX manuscripts that have come down to us. As we will see later, Matthew appears to know a text that differs considerably from any known Greek or Hebrew text. See further, Jennifer M. Dines, *The Septuagint* (London: T. & T. Clark, 2004).

3 See Morna D. Hooker, *Beginnings: Keys that Open the Gospel* (London: SCM, 1997).

4 See Clive Marsh and S. Moyise, *Jesus and the Gospels* (2nd edn; London: T. & T. Clark, 2006).

5 Wrede's book was first published in German in 1901 as *Das Messiasgeheimnis in den Evangelien*, and became available in English as *The Messianic Secret* (Cambridge: James Clarke, 1971).

6 First published in German as *Von Reimarus zu Wrede* in 1906, it was translated as *The Quest of the Historical Jesus* and went through six editions, sometimes with significant changes. The latest and only complete edition in English was published by SCM in 2000 (edited by John Bowden).

7 Charles H. Dodd, *Historical Tradition in the Fourth Gospel* (Cambridge: Cambridge University Press, 1963); John A. T. Robinson, *The Priority of John* (ed. J. F. Coakley; London: SCM, 1985).

8 For an introduction to Q, see Mark Goodacre, *The Synoptic Problem: A Way Through the Maze* (London: Continuum, 2001), though it should be noted that Goodacre does not himself believe in the existence of Q as a single document.

1 Jesus and Scripture according to Mark's Gospel

1 James Crossley thinks that a particular tradition is in mind, whereby impurity can pass from hands to food via liquid. Jesus denies this and Mark draws the conclusion that all foods, that is, everything permitted by the law, remain clean. See James D. Crossley, *The Date of Mark's Gospel:*

Insight from the Law in Earliest Christianity (JSNTSup, 266; London & New York: T. & T. Clark, 2004), pp. 228–31; J. Svartvik, *Mark and Mission: Mark 7:1-23 in its Narrative and Historical Contexts* (ConBNT, 32; Stockholm: Almqvist & Wiksell International, 2000).

2 John P. Meier, *A Marginal Jew: Rethinking the Historical Jesus. Vol. 3: Companions and Competitors* (New Haven, CT: Yale University Press, 2007), pp. 429–30.

3 John P. Meier, *A Marginal Jew: Rethinking the Historical Jesus. Vol. 4: Law and Love* (New Haven, CT: Yale University Press, 2009), p. 113.

4 This is the most likely meaning of the phrase 'in their lifetimes', that is, the man's lifetime. However, since the word 'women' comes immediately before the phrase, it has been argued that the reference is to the woman's lifetime (despite the masculine suffix). If this is the case, then it is polygamy rather than divorce that is being condemned.

5 William R. G. Loader, *Jesus' Attitude to the Law* (WUNT, 2.97; Tübingen: Mohr Siebeck, 1997), p. 101.

6 Joachim Jeremias, *Parables of the Kingdom* (London: SCM, 1972), pp. 13–18.

7 William R. Telford, *The Theology of Mark* (Cambridge: Cambridge University Press, 1999), p. 66.

8 E. P. Sanders, *Jewish Law from Jesus to the Mishnah: Five Studies* (London: SCM/Philadelphia, PA: Trinity, 1990), pp. 84–96. See also John Bowker, *Jesus and the Pharisees* (Cambridge: Cambridge University Press, 2008); John P. Meier, *A Marginal Jew: Rethinking the Historical Jesus. Vol. 3: Companions and Competitors* (New Haven, CT: Yale University Press, 2007), pp. 289–388.

9 Morna D. Hooker, *Jesus the Servant* (London: SPCK, 1959).

10 Richard T. France, *The Gospel of Mark* (NIGTC; Grand Rapids, MI: Eerdmans, 2002), pp. 500–1. It should be noted that France does not think the Church was wrong to speak of Jesus' second coming, for he believes this is the meaning of Mark 13.32: 'But about that day or hour no one knows, neither the angels in heaven, nor the Son, but only the father.'

11 The early Greek manuscripts contained almost no punctuation and never the equivalent of our question mark. It is only from the context that we can decide whether we are dealing with a statement or a question.

12 Joel Marcus, *The Way of the Lord: Christological Exegesis of the Old Testament in the Gospel of Mark* (Edinburgh: T. & T. Clark, 1992), pp. 94–110. Marcus calls it a 'Refutational Form' and illustrates it from the Jewish midrashic work known as the Mekilta.

13 France, *Gospel of Mark*, p. 359.

14 Marcus, *Way of the Lord*, pp. 149–50.

15 France, *Gospel of Mark*, pp. 62–3.

16 See further J. Samuel Subramanian, *The Synoptic Gospels and the Psalms as Prophecy* (London and New York: T. & T. Clark, 2007).

17 The ambiguity of Mark's Gospel has lent itself to 'postmodern' interpretation, where words simultaneously communicate and distort meaning. The message of Mark, on this understanding, is that human categories, even those derived from the Scriptures, cannot encapsulate the significance of Jesus. See George Aichele, *Jesus Framed* (New York: Routledge, 1996).

2 Jesus and Scripture according to Matthew's Gospel

1 James D. Crossley, *The Date of Mark's Gospel: Insight from the Law in Earliest Christianity* (JSNTSup, 266; London and New York: T. & T. Clark, 2004).

2 However, in a different setting (Matt. 23.16–22), Jesus challenges the scribal distinctions between swearing by the sanctuary and swearing by the gold of the sanctuary, without forbidding oaths altogether. This could represent a different viewpoint, but it is more likely that Matthew thinks that on this occasion, Jesus was content to expose the fallacy of their reasoning.

3 The exception is James 5.12: 'Above all, my beloved, do not swear, either by heaven or by earth or by any other oath, but let your "Yes" be yes and your "No" be no, so that you may not fall under condemnation.' This shows that at least one Christian community tried to follow Jesus here, and so it is not quite true to say that it is unknown in the early Church. However, differences in wording suggest that James is an independent witness to this tradition, which adds to the case for authenticity. John Meier says: 'Jesus' shocking teaching, which presumed to revoke some institution or command of the Mosaic Law, probably evoked no little dissent and debate among his Jewish listeners' (*A Marginal Jew: Rethinking the Historical Jesus. Vol. 4: Law and Love* (New Haven, CT: Yale University Press, 2009), p. 205.

4 Meier, *Law and Love*, pp. 499–522.

5 The verb 'hang' is in the singular (corrected in later manuscripts) and might suggest that Matthew originally had only 'law' in mind but decided to add 'prophets' as an afterthought. This is the view of Robert H. Gundry, *Matthew: A Commentary on His Handbook for a Mixed Church under Persecution* (2nd edn; Grand Rapids, MI: Eerdmans, 1994), p. 450. He adds: 'We need not dispute whether "hang" means that all the other commandments can be deduced from these two or whether these commandments summarize all the others, for what summarizes the others also provides a starting point for deduction . . . Either way, love for God and neighbour must permeate obedience to all the other commandments' (p. 450).

6 For an introduction to the issues, see Timothy R. McLay, *The Use of the Septuagint in New Testament Research* (Grand Rapids, MI: Eerdmans, 2003).

7 Not least that he attributes the saying to Jeremiah. It would appear that Matthew has considerably reworded Zechariah 11.12–13 and combined it with phrases from Jeremiah 18.2–3 and perhaps also Jeremiah 32.6–15.

8 Clay Alan Ham, *The Coming King and the Rejected Shepherd: Matthew's Reading of Zechariah's Messianic Hope* (Sheffield: Sheffield Phoenix Press, 2005), p. 126.

9 N. T. Wright, *Christian Origins and the Question of God. Vol. 2: Jesus and the Victory of God* (London: SPCK/Minneapolis, MN: Fortress Press, 1996), p. 535. Wright considers this to go back to Jesus and so represents a messianic consciousness of his own role.

10 The NRSV includes a footnote saying, 'Other ancient authorities lack verse 44'. It is present in the majority of manuscripts but since it occurs in Luke's version of the story (Luke 20.18), there is the suspicion that an early copyist might have mistakenly added it. If this is so, then our discussion of it should be transferred to Luke.

11 Though the Aramaic Targum that has come down to us also uses 'Eli' in this instance.

12 J. Samuel Subramanian, *The Synoptic Gospels and the Psalms as Prophecy* (London and New York: T. & T. Clark, 2007), p. 99.

13 Gundry thinks that the Hebrew word *oz*, which is usually translated 'strength', can mean something like 'praise' in certain settings (e.g. Ps. 29.1). If this is the case then Matthew has removed the ambiguity by following the LXX's *ainon* ('praise'). See Robert H. Gundry, *The Use of the Old Testament in St. Matthew's Gospel with Special Reference to the Messianic Hope* (NovTSup, 18; Leiden: Brill, 1967), p. 121.

14 Gundry, *Matthew*, p. 414.

15 Subramanian, *The Synoptic Gospels*, p. 118. So also Gundry, *Matthew*, pp. 473–4. A different view comes from Dale Allison who argues that the 'until' should not be taken in a temporal sense ('when') but as a conditional ('if'): 'Jesus affirms that, if she will, Jerusalem can, in the end, bless in the name of the Lord the one who will come, and her doing so, that is, her repentance, will lead to deliverance' (p. 80). See Dale C. Allison, 'Matthew 23:29 = Luke 13:35b as a Conditional Prophecy', *JSNT* 18 (1983), pp. 75–84.

3 Jesus and Scripture according to Luke's Gospel

1 The most significant are the so-called 'minor agreements', where Matthew and Luke agree against Mark. On the theory that Matthew and Luke expanded Mark independently, these agreements can only be explained

by coincidence or that they were present in Q. Although the agreements are usually just odd words (hence 'minor'), there are a lot of them, making it virtually impossible to put down to coincidence. On the other hand, if each of these comes from Q, then the rationale for Q diminishes, since it must share a good number of stories with Mark.

2 John P. Meier, *A Marginal Jew: Rethinking the Historical Jesus. Vol. 4: Law and Love* (New Haven, CT: Yale University Press, 2009), p. 296.

3 Steven M. Bryan, *Jesus and Israel's Traditions of Judgement and Restoration* (SNTSMS 117; Cambridge: Cambridge University Press, 2002), p. 182, developing the argument of Richard J. Bauckham, 'The Scrupulous Priest and the Good Samaritan: Jesus' Parabolic Interpretation of the Law of Moses', *NTS* 44 (1998), pp. 475–89.

4 William R. G. Loader, *Jesus' Attitude to the Law* (WUNT, 2.97; Tübingen: Mohr Siebeck, 1997), p. 327.

5 James D. Crossley, *The Date of Mark's Gospel: Insight from the Law in Earliest Christianity* (JSNTSup, 266; London & New York: T. & T. Clark, 2004), pp. 117–20.

6 James M. Robinson, P. Hoffmann and J. S. Kloppenborg, *The Critical Edition of Q* (Leuven: Peeters/Minneapolis, MN: Fortress, 2000).

7 The question of whether there was a fixed lectionary of readings at this point is extremely complex, and indeed this story is one of the earliest pieces of evidence. From later sources we know that the pattern was to begin with a reading from the law and follow it with a reading from the prophets, but we do not know when this was standardized for all synagogues. For an attempt to reconstruct such a lectionary, see J. Mann, *The Bible as Read and Preached in the Old Synagogue* (New York: KTAV, 1971).

8 This is most clearly seen in the phrase 'recovery of sight to the blind', where the Hebrew text speaks of 'release to the prisoners'.

9 Charles A. Kimball, *Jesus' Exposition of the Old Testament in Luke* (Sheffield: Sheffield Academic Press, 1994), p. 110.

10 Michael Prior, *Jesus the Liberator: Nazareth Liberation Theology* (Sheffield: Sheffield Academic Press, 1995).

11 It is interesting to note that in the sayings about discipleship and service, both Matthew and Mark end with the saying, 'the Son of Man came not to be served but to serve, and to give his life a ransom for many' (Mark 10.45/Matt. 20.27). This is missing from Luke's version of the story, and some scholars have suggested that Luke does not wish to propagate a substitutionary understanding of atonement.

12 Christopher F. Evans, *Saint Luke* (London: SCM, 1990), p. 688.

13 Kimball, *Jesus' Exposition*, p. 163. In this context, '*pesher*-like' means that the form resembles the way that the Qumran commentaries (known as *pesherim*) interpret Scripture.

14 So Evans, *Saint Luke*, p. 877.

15 N. T. Wright, *Christian Origins and the Question of God. Vol. 2: Jesus and the Victory of God* (London: SPCK/Minneapolis, MN: Fortress Press, 1996), p. 594.

4 Jesus and Scripture according to John's Gospel

1 See Craig Blomberg, *The Historical Reliability of the Gospels* (revised edn; Downers Grove, IL: IVP, 2008); Richard J. Bauckham, *Jesus and the Eyewitnesses: The Gospel as Eyewitness Testimony* (Grand Rapids, MI: Eerdmans, 2008).

2 Peder Borgen, *Bread from Heaven: An Exegetical Study of the Concept of Manna in the Gospel of John and the Writings of Philo* (Leiden: Brill, 1965).

3 Maarten J. J. Menken, *Old Testament Quotations in the Fourth Gospel: Studies in Textual Form* (Kampen: Kok, 1996).

4 Rudolf Bultmann, *The Gospel of John* (Oxford: Blackwell, 1971), p. 389.

5 Anthony T. Hanson, *The Prophetic Gospel: A Study of John and the Old Testament* (Edinburgh: T. & T. Clark, 1991), pp. 144–9.

6 Menken argues that John would hardly wish to use a quotation that suggests that Jesus was betrayed 'by craftiness' and hence translated the Hebrew for himself. However, he believes that the expression 'lifting the heel' (both Greek and Hebrew have 'magnifying') is an allusion to the betrayal of David by Ahithophel (2 Sam. 18.28). Both plan to do the deed at night and both hang themselves after the deed is done. Furthermore, both Jesus and David pray for deliverance on the Mount of Olives (2 Sam. 15.31/Mark 14.26ff.), and the Kidron valley is specifically mentioned in John 18.1 (cf. 2 Sam. 15.23).

7 The Hebrew text of Zechariah 14.21 is ambiguous since 'trader' has the same consonants as 'Canaanite'. The LXX took it as 'Canaanite', and that is how it is rendered in KJV/NIV. However, NRSV/NJB render it 'traders'.

8 N. T. Wright, *Christian Origins and the Question of God. Vol. 2: Jesus and the Victory of God* (London: SPCK/Minneapolis, MN: Fortress Press, 1996), p. 645.

5 Jesus and Scripture – minimalist views

1 The text is taken from H. Bettenson, *Documents of the Christian Church* (2nd edn; Oxford: Oxford University Press, 1963), pp. 51–2 (format altered).

2 W. Wrede, *The Messianic Secret* (Cambridge: James Clarke, 1971). See Introduction, note 5, for the German title.

3 It is interesting that Luke decided to keep the command to silence (Luke 8.56), but the words 'he ordered them to tell no one what had happened' probably refer to *how* Jesus brought her back to life rather than the fact of it.

4 Geza Vermes, *Jesus the Jew: A Historian's Reading of the Gospels* (London: Collins, 1973).

5 Geza Vermes, *The Authentic Gospel of Jesus* (London: Penguin Books, 2003), p. 174.

6 Vermes, *Authentic Gospel*, p. 280.

7 C. E. B. Cranfield, *St Mark* (Cambridge: Cambridge University Press, 1959), pp. 272–6.

8 Vermes, *Authentic Gospel*, p. 53. He cites the judgement of the Mishnah in *m. Nedarim* 3:2: 'If a man saw (from a distance) people eating his figs and said, "May they be Corban to you!" and they were found to be his father and brothers and others with them, the School of Shammai say, "For them (father and brothers) the vow is not binding, but for the others with them it is binding." And the School of Hillel say, "For neither of them is binding"' (p. 54).

9 Based on Vermes, *Authentic Gospel*, pp. 376–89.

10 Vermes, *Authentic Gospel*, pp. 401, 402, 403, 408.

11 John Dominic Crossan, *The Historical Jesus: The Life of a Mediterranean Jewish Peasant* (Edinburgh: T. & T. Clark, 1991), p. 422. In his summary of Crossan's thought, Mark Allan Powell says that it 'does not wait for God to act violently to judge the world but assumes God is waiting for us to act nonviolently to redeem it'. See Mark Allan Powell, *Jesus as a Figure in History: How Modern Historians View the Man from Galilee* (Louisville, KY: John Knox, 1998), p. 91.

12 John S. Kloppenborg, *The Formation of Q: Trajectories in Ancient Wisdom Collections* (Philadelphia, PA: Fortress, 1987).

13 Text quoted from the translation in Kloppenborg et al., *Q Thomas Reader* (Sonoma, CA: Polebridge Press, 1990). See also Helmut Koester, *Ancient Christian Gospels: Their History and Development* (London: SCM/ Philadelphia, PA: Trinity Press, 1990).

14 The Cynic movement probably originated with Diogenes of Sinope (400–325 BCE). In Powell's words (*Jesus as a Figure in History*, pp. 60–1), they were 'radical individualists who advocated the avoidance of worldly entanglements and defiance of social convention ... They dressed as beggars with a cloak, bag, and staff, wore their hair long and kept their beards untrimmed.'

15 Quoted in Crossan, *Historical Jesus*, p. 266.

16 Crossan, *Historical Jesus*, p. 269.

17 Marcus J. Borg, *Conflict, Holiness, and Politics in the Teachings of Jesus* (revised edn; Harrisburg, PA: Trinity Press, 1998), p. 247.

18 Borg, *Conflict, Holiness, and Politics*, p. 165.

19 Borg, *Conflict, Holiness, and Politics*, pp. 162, 173: 'In none of these cases did the healing seem to be a strategic suspension of sabbath law,

as neither danger to life nor particular exigencies of the mission were involved. Instead, these violations of sabbath law as then understood seem to be programmatic, flowing out of the alternative paradigm which Jesus taught: the sabbath was a day for works of compassion. This change did not mean that the sabbath was abrogated; rather it was subordinated to deeds of compassion rather than to the quest for holiness' (p. 162).

20 Borg, *Conflict, Holiness, and Politics*, p. 186, n. 55.

21 Borg, *Conflict, Holiness, and Politics*, p. 15. He adds that while the Pharisees were not formally connected with the temple, their emphasis on purity and tithing is in fact a sharing of that ideology. By their emphasis on holiness as separation they support and legitimate the domination system.

22 Borg, *Conflict, Holiness, and Politics*, p. 220.

6 Jesus and Scripture – moderate views

1 See the chapter on sources in James D. G. Dunn, *Christianity in the Making. Vol. 1: Jesus Remembered* (Grand Rapids, MI: Eerdmans, 2003), pp. 139–72.

2 The parallels with the Aramaic Targum are used as a sign of authenticity in Bruce Chilton, *A Galilean Rabbi and His Bible: Jesus' Own Interpretation of Isaiah* (London: SPCK, 1984); Craig A. Evans, *To See and Not Perceive: Isaiah 6.9-10 in Early Jewish and Christian Interpretation* (JSOTSup 64; Sheffield: Sheffield Academic Press, 1989). It is denied by Michael D. Goulder, 'Those Outside (Mark 4.10–12)', *NovT* 33 (1991), pp. 289–302.

3 John P. Meier, *A Marginal Jew: Rethinking the Historical Jesus. Vol. 2: Mentor, Message, and Miracles* (New York: Doubleday, 1994), p. 141.

4 N. T. Wright, *Christian Origins and the Question of God. Vol. 2: Jesus and the Victory of God* (London: SPCK/Minneapolis, MN: Fortress Press, 1996), pp. 612–53.

5 E. P. Sanders, *Jesus and Judaism* (London: SCM, 1985), pp. 98–106. Some have thought that the differences between the lists of the twelve (Matt. 10.2–4; Mark 3.16–19; Luke 6.14–16; Acts 1.13) count against this, but Sanders argues that if the Church wanted to create the tradition that Jesus specifically chose 12 disciples, they would hardly have given them different names. The more likely explanation is that Jesus spoke about the 12, but the tradition was not clear on who precisely they were.

6 Sanders, *Jesus and Judaism*, p. 319.

7 Steven M. Bryan, *Jesus and Israel's Traditions of Judgement and Restoration* (SNTSMS 117; Cambridge: Cambridge University Press, 2002), p. 86.

8 The Hebrew word occurs 73 times in the Hebrew Bible, mostly in the historical books, where it refers to the Canaanites. However, in Job 40.30 and Proverbs 31.24 the context is buying and selling, and the word seems

to mean something like 'merchants'. The question is, what does it mean in Zech. 14.21? The LXX (NETS) took it as 'Canaanites'.

9 Craig A. Evans, 'Jesus and Zechariah's Messianic Hope', in Bruce Chilton and C. A. Evans (eds), *Authenticating the Activities of Jesus* (Leiden: Brill, 1999), pp. 373–88.

10 Intertextuality is the name given to a broad number of theories concerning how texts relate to other texts. They generally agree that such relationships are complex, so that a quotation or allusion to one text necessarily has an effect on the interpretation of related texts. In the present example, scholars have explained Mark 13.26 as an interpretation of Daniel 7.13, without realizing that their understanding of Daniel 7.13 has been influenced by their interpretation of Mark 13.26. See my *Evoking Scripture: Seeing the Old Testament in the New* (London and New York: T. & T. Clark, 2008).

11 Morna D. Hooker, *The Son of Man in Mark* (London: SPCK, 1967), p. 192.

12 Hooker, *The Son of Man in Mark*, p. 192.

13 Only in Stephen's speech in Acts 7.56, the quotation of Psalm 8 in Hebrews 2.6ff. and the allusion to Daniel 7.13 in Revelation 1.13.

14 E. P. Sanders, *Jewish Law from Jesus to the Mishnah: Five Studies* (London: SCM/Philadelphia, PA: Trinity, 1990), p. 90.

15 Tom Holmén, *Jesus and Jewish Covenant Thinking* (Leiden: Brill, 2001), p. 180.

16 Holmén, *Jesus and Jewish Covenant Thinking*, p. 169.

17 James D. Crossley, *The Date of Mark's Gospel: Insight from the Law in Earliest Christianity* (JSNTSup, 266; London & New York: T. & T. Clark, 2004), p. 123.

18 James D. G. Dunn, *Christianity in the Making. Vol. 1: Jesus Remembered* (Grand Rapids, MI: Eerdmans, 2003), p. 336.

19 Dunn, *Jesus Remembered*, p. 569, drawing on Holmén, *Jesus and Jewish Covenant Thinking*.

20 Dunn, *Jesus Remembered*, p. 807.

21 Wright, *Jesus and the Victory of God*, p. 96.

22 Wright, *Jesus and the Victory of God*, pp. 126–7.

23 Wright, *Jesus and the Victory of God*, p. 132.

24 Wright, *Jesus and the Victory of God*, pp. 238–9.

25 Wright, *Jesus and the Victory of God*, p. 594.

26 Wright, *Jesus and the Victory of God*, p. 603.

7 Jesus and Scripture – maximalist views

1 I. Howard Marshall, *Luke: Historian and Theologian* (2nd edn; Grand Rapids, MI: Zondervan, 1989).

2 Charles A. Kimball, *Jesus' Exposition of the Old Testament in Luke* (Sheffield: Sheffield Academic Press, 1994), pp. 43–4.

3 Kimball, *Jesus' Exposition*, p. 96.

4 Kimball, *Jesus' Exposition*, pp. 114–15.

5 Kimball, *Jesus' Exposition*, p. 197.

6 A slightly modified summary of Kimball, *Jesus' Exposition*, pp. 57–8.

7 Richard T. France, *Jesus and the Old Testament: His Application of Old Testament Passages to Himself and His Mission* (London: Tyndale, 1971), p. 46.

8 France, *Jesus and the Old Testament*, pp. 227–36.

9 Although neatly solving the problem, many scholars doubt that the change from 'those days' to 'that day' is sufficient to indicate such a significant change of reference.

10 France, *Jesus and the Old Testament*, p. 127.

11 France, *Jesus and the Old Testament*, p. 132.

12 France, *Jesus and the Old Testament*, p. 93.

13 France, *Jesus and the Old Testament*, p. 109.

14 France, *Jesus and the Old Testament*, p. 226.

15 See my *Paul and Scripture* (London: SPCK, 2010) and *The Old Testament in the New* (London: T. & T. Clark, 2001).

16 France, *Jesus and the Old Testament*, p. 223.

Conclusion

1 Geza Vermes, *The Authentic Gospel of Jesus* (London: Penguin Books, 2003), p. 173.

2 I discuss this in the final chapter ('Literary and theological reflections') of my *Evoking Scripture: Seeing the Old Testament in the New* (London and New York: T. & T. Clark, 2008), pp. 125–41.

3 One might also note that since the Gospels are written in Greek, none of the recorded words were actually spoken by Jesus. What we have is a series of Greek sayings that seek to encapsulate Jesus' teaching. Sometimes there are good grounds for thinking that these are fairly literal translations of Aramaic sayings, but at other times they appear to be paraphrases or even summaries of his teaching. This offers a broader context for evaluating the validity of the Greek words of Luke 22.37, which might not correspond to any Aramaic saying spoken by Jesus but might accurately summarize his position.

Select bibliography

This select bibliography is divided into those works recommended for further reading, followed by those that are more technical (often using Greek and Hebrew) and that have been important in writing this book.

Further reading

Allison, Dale C., *The Historical Christ and the Theological Jesus* (Grand Rapids, MI: Eerdmans, 2009).

Borg, Marcus J., *Conflict, Holiness, and Politics in the Teachings of Jesus* (revised edn; Harrisburg, PA: Trinity Press, 1998).

Bowker, John, *Jesus and the Pharisees* (Cambridge: Cambridge University Press, 2008).

Crossan, John Dominic, *The Historical Jesus: The Life of a Mediterranean Jewish Peasant* (Edinburgh: T. & T. Clark, 1991).

Crossley, James G., *The New Testament and Jewish Law: A Guide for the Perplexed* (London and New York: T. & T. Clark, 2010).

Dunn, James D. G., *Christianity in the Making. Vol. 1: Jesus Remembered* (Grand Rapids, MI: Eerdmans, 2003).

Goodacre, Mark, *The Synoptic Problem: A Way Through the Maze* (London: Continuum, 2001).

Kloppenborg, John S. et al., *Q Thomas Reader* (Sonoma, CA: Polebridge Press, 1990).

McLay, Timothy R., *The Use of the Septuagint in New Testament Research* (Grand Rapids, MI: Eerdmans, 2003).

Marsh, Clive and S. Moyise, *Jesus and the Gospels* (2nd edn; London: T. & T. Clark, 2006).

Moyise, Steve, *The Old Testament in the New* (London: T. & T. Clark, 2001).

Moyise, Steve, *Evoking Scripture: Seeing the Old Testament in the New* (London and New York: T. & T. Clark, 2008).

Pietersma, Albert and B. G. Wright (eds), *A New English Translation of the Septuagint* (New York: Oxford University Press, 2007).

Powell, Mark Allan, *Jesus as a Figure in History: How Modern Historians View the Man from Galilee* (Louisville, KY: John Knox Press, 1998).

Sanders, E. P., *Jesus and Judaism* (London: SCM, 1985).

Vermes, Geza, *The Authentic Gospel of Jesus* (London: Penguin Books, 2003).

Wright, N. T., *Christian Origins and the Question of God. Vol. 1: The New Testament and the People of God* (London: SPCK/Minneapolis, MN: Fortress, 1992).

Wright, N. T., *Christian Origins and the Question of God. Vol. 2: Jesus and the Victory of God* (London: SPCK/Minneapolis, MN: Fortress Press, 1996).

More technical

Allison, Dale C., *The Intertextual Jesus: Scripture in Q* (Harrisburg, PA: Trinity, 2000).

Borgen, Peder, *Bread from Heaven: An Exegetical Study of the Concept of Manna in the Gospel of John and the Writings of Philo* (Leiden: Brill, 1965).

Bryan, Stephen M., *Jesus and Israel's Traditions of Judgement and Restoration* (SNTSMS 117; Cambridge: Cambridge University Press, 2002).

Dodd, Charles H., *Historical Tradition in the Fourth Gospel* (Cambridge: Cambridge University Press, 1963).

Chilton, Bruce, *A Galilean Rabbi and His Bible: Jesus' Own Interpretation of Isaiah* (London: SPCK, 1984).

Chilton, Bruce and C. A. Evans (eds), *Authenticating the Activities of Jesus* (Leiden: Brill, 1999).

Crossley, James D., *The Date of Mark's Gospel: Insight from the Law in Earliest Christianity* (JSNTSup, 266; London and New York: T. & T. Clark, 2004).

Evans, Craig A., *To See and Not Perceive: Isaiah 6.9-10 in Early Jewish and Christian Interpretation* (JSOTSup, 64; Sheffield: Sheffield Academic Press, 1989).

Evans, Craig A., 'Jesus and Zechariah's Messianic Hope', in Bruce Chilton and C. A. Evans (eds), *Authenticating the Activities of Jesus* (Leiden: Brill, 1999), pp. 373–88.

France, Richard T., *Jesus and the Old Testament: His Application of Old Testament Passages to Himself and His Mission* (London: Tyndale, 1971).

France, Richard T., *The Gospel of Mark* (NIGTC; Grand Rapids, MI: Eerdmans, 2002).

Gundry, Robert H., *The Use of the Old Testament in St. Matthew's Gospel with Special Reference to the Messianic Hope* (NovTSup, 18; Leiden: Brill, 1967).

Gundry, Robert H., *Matthew: A Commentary on His Handbook for a Mixed Church under Persecution* (2nd edn; Grand Rapids, MI: Eerdmans, 1994).

Ham, Clay Alan, *The Coming King and the Rejected Shepherd: Matthew's Reading of Zechariah's Messianic Hope* (Sheffield: Sheffield Phoenix Press, 2005).

Select bibliography

Hanson, Anthony T., *The Prophetic Gospel: A Study of John and the Old Testament* (Edinburgh: T. & T. Clark, 1991).

Holmén, Tom, *Jesus and Jewish Covenant Thinking* (Leiden: Brill, 2001).

Hooker, Morna D., *Jesus the Servant* (London: SPCK, 1959).

Hooker, Morna D., *The Son of Man in Mark* (London: SPCK, 1967).

Kimball, Charles A., *Jesus' Use of the Old Testament in Luke* (Sheffield: Sheffield Academic Press, 1994).

Kloppenborg, John S., *The Formation of Q: Trajectories in Ancient Wisdom Collections* (Philadelphia, PA: Fortress Press, 1987).

Koester, Helmut, *Ancient Christian Gospels: Their History and Development* (London: SCM/Philadelphia, PA: Trinity Press, 1990).

Loader, William R. G., *Jesus' Attitude to the Law* (WUNT, 2.97; Tübingen: Mohr Siebeck, 1997).

Marcus, Joel, *The Way of the Lord: Christological Exegesis of the Old Testament in the Gospel of Mark* (Edinburgh: T. & T. Clark, 1992).

Meier, John P., *A Marginal Jew: Rethinking the Historical Jesus. Vol. 1: The Roots of the Problem and the Person* (New York: Doubleday, 1991).

Meier, John P., *A Marginal Jew: Rethinking the Historical Jesus. Vol. 2: Mentor, Message, and Miracles* (New York: Doubleday, 1994).

Meier, John P., *A Marginal Jew: Rethinking the Historical Jesus. Vol. 3: Companions and Competitors* (New Haven, CT: Yale University Press, 2007).

Meier, John P., *A Marginal Jew: Rethinking the Historical Jesus. Vol. 4: Law and Love* (New Haven, CT: Yale University Press, 2009).

Menken, Maarten J. J., *Old Testament Quotations in the Fourth Gospel: Studies in Textual Form* (Kampen: Kok, 1996).

Sanders, E. P., *Jewish Law from Jesus to the Mishnah: Five Studies* (London: SCM/Philadelphia, PA: Trinity, 1990).

Schweitzer, Albert, *The Quest of the Historical Jesus* (revised edn; London: SCM, 2000).

Subramanian, J. Samuel, *The Synoptic Gospels and the Psalms as Prophecy* (London and New York: T. & T. Clark, 2007).

Svartvik, J., *Mark and Mission: Mark 7:1-23 in its Narrative and Historical Contexts* (ConBNT, 32; Stockholm: Almqvist & Wiksell International, 2000).

Index of biblical references

Index of biblical references

Index of authors and subjects